Travel Bites

By

The Hungry Traveller

Wattle Publishing

Wattle Publishing Ltd
Third Floor, 207 Regent Street
London W1B 3HH
www.wattlepublishing.com

Published in Great Britain by Wattle Publishing Ltd in 2013
Copyright © 2012 by The Hungry Traveller
The moral right of the author has been asserted
www.travelbitesbythehungrytraveller.com

A catalogue record of this book is available from the British Library
ISBN 978-1-908959-13-3

Printed and Bound by CPI Group (UK) Ltd, Croydon, CRO 4YY

Dedication

This is dedicated to the many people whom I have met along the way and who have made my traveling experiences so memorable. From the local shopkeeper or train passenger who I met and passed a few hours with, to those people who through a chance meeting, I have formed life-long friendships. All of you have contributed to the episodes that have made this book possible.

Contents

Prologue

I never set out to write a book.

And no doubt, critics will say that I still haven't after they have read this.

It all started with a writing course in which we were assigned the task of writing about a memorable experience. I wrote about eating camel burgers in Meknes in Morocco. I enjoyed writing the story because the memory of my travels suddenly came alive, and this acted as a catalyst for remembering other events that I had almost forgotten. During the time I had been traveling, I had lacked the interest and self-discipline to keep a travel diary, so I jotted down all of the events that I could remember on a page. When I looked at the list that I had compiled, I found that, like the story of eating the camel burger, many of my memories and experiences were linked to food!

So that I would not completely forget these experiences, I started to write them down as a series of short stories, like a retrospective diary. What was most interesting was the importance of food, either as the center of the story itself or as the gateway into experiencing another culture. All of the recipes are from dishes that I now cook but had mostly never even tried (let alone cooked) until my travels.

Most of my stories cover a span of over fifteen years and are reflections of my experiences from visiting different places. Reading some of these stories, you can probably tell that some of these episodes affected me on a more personal level than others. But I guess it is all of life's experiences, both good and bad, that make us into the people who we become.

I am sure that in the intervening years, a lot of things may have changed in many of the places I have visited. It would be great if you shared your travel experiences, or perhaps how things have changed from what I have described in the book on my blog (www.travelbitesbythehungrytraveller.com) or on twitter (@travel_bites). I always like to read about other peoples' travel experiences.

Finally, this book does not claim to be an academic text. Any facts or information that I have included in each travel bite is based on information that I have picked up from local tour guides, museums and hearsay. Where possible, I have researched information to ensure that my stories are materially correct, but again, all feedback is welcome.

Also, if you follow any of my recipes, please make sure that none of the ingredients will trigger an allergic reaction before attempting the recipe.

I hope you enjoy my stories.

The Hungry Traveller

My First Day

Location: Ho Chi Minh City, Vietnam

My tentative smile was met by a stern expression from the immigration official who held up my passport opened at its photo page. She stared at me hard in the face and glanced from the photo to my face and back again several times. My smile quickly dropped as she went page by page through my passport, looking for my visa. Having found the correct page, she stamped my passport, handed it back to me, and nodded.

I was now on my way!

I moved past the immigration desk and started walking through the airport building. I was now buzzing. Only six weeks earlier I had made the relatively impulsive decision to buy a multi-stop plane ticket and give notice at work. Although I had been organized enough to buy myself a new backpack, I had done all of my packing at the last minute, not even thirty-six hours earlier. I had no idea when I would be back home.

More than ten years later, I still don't know.

As the plane touched down on the runway at Tan Son Nhat airport, I looked out of the window and to my surprise, saw old battle-scarred concrete bunkers along the side of the runway. It almost felt like a cliché, given that I had arrived in Ho Chi

Minh City in Vietnam. This city had formerly been known as Saigon before it was renamed in 1976, after the fall of the South Vietnamese government and the creation of the unified Vietnamese state.

After I left the terminal building, I finally felt like I was in Vietnam and that my adventure had begun! Through a lack of planning on my part, I had arrived during one of the hottest times of the year. I began to immediately perspire with the weight of the pack on my back. I sweltered under the baking hot sun, and the very high humidity caused the air to feel thick, magnifying the effect of the heat.

The airport was not that far from the center of the city so I decided I would splash out and get a taxi, rather than spend any more time than I had to walking around with my heavy backpack in the sun. I was one of the last people to come off my flight so I felt confident of my chances of not getting ripped off by the taxi drivers (I knew from the guidebook that taxis in Ho Chi Minh City are metered and that you should refuse to get into a taxi unless the driver switches on the meter).

Rather than sitting in their cars and taking their turns in the taxi stand, the drivers were directly approaching tourists for their business.

"Taxi? Taxi? Taxi?" they clamored.

"OK, but we use the taximeter." I replied.

With that over half of the drivers walked away without saying another word. The other half point blank refused.

"No taximeter! Twenty US dollar."

"No, taximeter!" I insisted.

After about fifteen minutes, the high handed advice in

the guidebook was just sounding like a whole lot of theory, written by someone who had never attempted to get a taxi from the airport where all of the drivers appeared to have formed a cartel. I was clearly going to have to make the most of a bad situation.

"Taxi? Taxi? Taxi?"

The call came from one of the few drivers left whom I had not already turned away.

"Yes. You use the taximeter?"

By now my voice had become more hopeful than assertive. Instead, I heard the now familiar

"Twenty US dollar."

I groaned inwardly. I had not really haggled for anything in years and was not really up for the challenge. But I had to try. Twenty dollars was a lot of money for me.

"That is too much!"

The driver laughed.

"Twenty dollar fixed price!"

This was going to be tough.

"Really? I see ten drivers and only one tourist."

By now, everyone else from my flight appeared to have begrudgingly paid over their twenty dollars so that they could be on their way. My comment made the driver hesitate and look around. I lowered my voice so that only he could hear,

"Ten dollars. Final offer. I will wait. Someone will take my money."

Over twenty-four hours of travel had made me a bit tetchy, but it seemed to work in my favor. The driver looked around again and wavered,

"Fifteen dollar."

"No, ten dollars. It is OK. I will ask another driver."

I got up to leave.

"OK. Ten US dollar."

I followed the driver to his taxi. Fortunately, it was not too far away. He went to open the trunk for my backpack.

"It is OK. I will carry it with me."

The taxi driver shrugged, got into his seat, and left me to manage as I squirmed into the front passenger seat.

"Which hotel?"

That was an excellent question. The guidebook, which I read before I left, had confidently made the assertion that there was an abundance of budget accommodation, and that the best thing to do was to turn up in the Pham Ngu Lao area and go from place to place. This way I could see the room first-hand and haggle down the price.

I tried to pronounce *Pham Ngu Lao*. However, Vietnamese is a tonal language, so I just got a confused look from the taxi driver. I dug out my guidebook and pointed to the written text. He smiled and nodded.

"*Pham Ngu Lao!*"

I thought that was what I had said.

We were finally off.

Ironically, the driver switched on his taximeter as if to taunt me and show just how much he was going to rip me off on the trip.

However, to be fair, he was actually a pretty friendly guy and was keen to strike up a conversation.

"You very hot!"

I was already sweating profusely before I got into the car. Although he had switched on the air conditioning, the car must have been sitting in the sun for some time, because it was stiflingly hot when I got in. The fact that I was nursing my backpack (although given its size, I was gripping it in more of a bear hug), and that the hot sun kept beating relentlessly through the glass, did little to help my situation. From behind my backpack I managed a muffled

"Yeah."

He then tapped the dashboard of the car.

"Very hot today."

I craned my neck around my pack. He was tapping a dashboard thermometer. It read 39°C (close enough to 100°F). All I could manage was another muffled

"Yeah."

I tried to look out the window. The roads were full of traffic. But most of the traffic consisted of motorcycles and scooters swerving in and out of imaginary lanes. And the bikes weren't just carrying single passengers. One scooter was carrying a family of four! Other bikes were basically working as delivery vans and were stacked up with goods. Yet despite the apparently random movement of traffic, it kept flowing (albeit not at the fastest pace). For a large city, there were a lot of trees growing along the side of the road. Curiously, almost all of the tree trunks were painted white.

Soon the taxi pulled up to the curb. We had arrived. The taximeter read a little over 40,000 dong. Despite my haggling, I had still managed to pay roughly three times too much. I handed the driver ten dollars, thanked him, and got out.

As the taxi pulled back into the traffic, I eased my backpack onto my shoulders. It seemed to be getting heavier.

I was also getting hotter and thirstier. The guidebook had assured me that I should be able to find a decent single room for six dollars a night. First up was an air-conditioned motel that offered me a room for ten dollars and would not negotiate on the price. I left and walked further down the road, where it was a similar situation at the next two places.

For the second time within an hour, I started to question the wisdom of paying too much attention to the guidebook. In theory, I could spend all day walking from place to place and no doubt find a decent place to stay for six dollars a night. However, the practicalities of doing that after not sleeping for over twenty-four hours and carrying a heavy pack in the blistering heat had me swearing at the authors of the book.

I had almost walked around the entire block. I was feeling tired, hot, and really annoyed with myself for not having booked somewhere to stay for at least my first night. By now I should have been sitting somewhere with air-conditioning and enjoying a cold beer. The next place I arrived at was apparently a family guesthouse. This much I only knew because a kid leaning in the doorway asked if I was looking for somewhere to stay. There was no sign above the doorway.

I followed him along a darkened corridor which opened into some sort of living room area where he introduced me to the landlady, who could not speak English. He explained that the landlady had two rooms, but that the larger one had already been taken for the night. However, they could show me the smaller room.

It was not a small room, it was tiny. It was an internal room and only a little bigger than the single bed that occupied it. Yet bizarrely, it had an en suite toilet and shower. Although there were no windows, it did have a small fan.

"How much?"

"Four US dollars."

"I'll take it!"

I handed over four single notes to the landlady, who in return handed me the key to the door. I had had enough. I was exhausted from the heat and lack of sleep. And besides, how bad could it be for one night?

I closed and locked the door behind me, remembering to switch on the light so that I would not be in complete darkness. There was barely enough space for me to stand in the room. I sat down on the bed next to my pack. It felt even hotter inside the room than outside on the street. I switched on the fan, which only managed to circulate the hot air, and took a shower. At least that was cold!

Lying back on the bed afterwards, I tried to get some sleep. But after a fitful hour, the heat of the room was too much, and now feeling hot, tired, thirsty, and hungry, I decided to go for a walk around the area.

It was now around midday and although the sun was hotter, walking around without a backpack did make a huge difference. I also found that if I walked at a slow enough pace, like the locals were doing, it also reduced the impact of the humidity. Before long, I walked past a shop selling chicken pho (noodle soup). I only really knew this because there was a price list in English in the window. In the front of the shop there was a huge cauldron of steaming broth and I noticed that as people placed their orders, the cooks would put some noodles and chicken pieces into a wire cage and drop it into the pot. After a few minutes, the basket would be lifted out, the noodles and chicken would be placed into a bowl and some broth from the large pot would be ladled over the top.

Most of the customers were Vietnamese, and the shop offered a choice of what part of the chicken you wanted: breast, leg, thigh, wing, liver, or offal. I had enough friends who had grown in South East Asia and China to know that offal, liver, and meat on the bone would be preferred to breast meat locally, so seeing most of the baskets being cooked with chicken livers, offal, or the occasional thigh, came as no real surprise. However, what surprised me was the popularity of these cuts, given that they cost up to fifty per cent more than the cheapest part of the chicken available, the breast.

The food looked good and the place seemed to be rather popular, so I went in. I walked up to the counter and ordered my food by raising four fingers, the number on the menu that corresponded to noodle soup with breast meat. Given that the shop was so close to the back packer area, the people who worked there were no doubt used to clueless tourists, and the lady taking my order seemed to understand what I was trying to ask for with a minimum of fuss. I also grabbed a large bottle of water and paid for my lunch.

A few minutes later, a steaming bowl was handed to me. I chose a stool at a bench that faced the street so that I could people-watch while I ate. As I expected, the broth was quite tasty but I struggled to pick up the vermicelli noodles with my chopsticks. However, given that everyone around me was busily slurping on their noodles, I did not feel so bad having to do the same.

After eating my food and drinking a lot of water I felt much better, so I continued with my walk. However, I soon found myself in trouble, as I came to my first busy road, where there was a constant stream of traffic. Although I was at a crossing that occasionally showed a green pedestrian light, traffic would continue to flow past. A cyclo driver, who had been watching me for a few minutes, took pity on me and came up to offer some advice.

"You cannot wait for no traffic. There is always traffic. You just walk and don't stop."

The look I gave him in response to this piece of advice, probably gave the impression that I thought he was insane.

"OK. Come with me."

Waiting for a small gap in the traffic so we would not be immediately run down, he stepped off the curve and began pushing his cyclo across the road. I started walking with him. I noticed that once he started to walk across the road he no longer paid any attention to the traffic around him. I was not so blasé. However, as we moved across the road, I noticed that the motorcycle traffic just weaved around us. Once we had passed halfway and the traffic was now coming straight towards me, he saw my hesitation and called out,

"Keep walk! Keep walk! You stop. You get hit!"

That was all the motivation I needed to keep going. Then, and I thought rather unnecessarily, he added,

"They more scared of damage hitting you"

I turned, expecting him to be laughing at his joke, but surprisingly, he seemed to be quite serious.

Once we had safely crossed, I thanked him for his help. Then came the sales pitch I had been expecting.

"Have you been on cyclo before?"

"No."

I tried to appear slightly uninterested. In reality, as soon as I had first seen one in the taxi trip over, I had wanted to have a ride in a cyclo! For the uninitiated, the cyclo looks like a reverse tricycle. A single passenger sits in a low, open front seat and the driver pedals the cyclo sitting to the rear and looking over the head of the passenger.

"I take you on city tour. All afternoon only 100,000 dong"

I may have wanted to go on a trip in a cyclo, but even I could see that this was a lot of money to ask. And besides, I knew that you should never accept the first offer.

"So where will you take me?"

"Reunification Palace, War Remnants Museum…"

I interrupted him.

"I have seen these already."

I know this was a lie, but all of these locations were within walking distance and I had planned to see them the next day. There was a pause as the driver thought of a new plan.

"Ok, I take you to Jade Emperor Pagoda and Thien Hau Pagoda"

I had no plans to visit these temples, so this seemed like a pretty good idea.

"But what is your best price?"

After a few minutes of negotiation, we agreed on a price of 50,000 dong. Even to this day I still have no idea whether this was a good price for the two hours or so spent cycling around that afternoon.

I sat down on the passenger seat. With an audible groan, the driver pushed off. It sounded like the bicycle powering the cyclo did not have any gears. Fortunately, the city is really flat. Riding in the cyclo was an amazing experience. It has to be one of the best ways to see the city, as you are sitting at ground level and are in among all of the city's sights, sounds, colors and people. However, I will admit that every time the driver had to turn across the traffic my heart was in my mouth. Bikes and even cars would stream straight towards me, as the cyclo slowly turned across their line of travel, and I sat there in a completely unprotected, open seat hoping that they would weave around us!

The temples themselves were interesting. The Thien Hau Pagoda is dedicated to a sea goddess called Lady Thien Hau. However, my personal favorite was the Jade Emperor Pagoda, which is dedicated to the supreme Taoist god. From the courtyard pool full of turtles to the effigies and carvings, which ranged from depictions of hell to a life-size effigy of a horse, it all appeared to be fairly eclectic to someone with no understanding of the religion or the symbolism. The strong pungent smoky haze from the burning joss sticks just added to the mystique of the place.

The cyclo driver, who had been waiting outside the gates while I went in, couldn't really enlighten me much either as to what I was seeing.

It was difficult to chat with the cyclo driver while we were on the move. As he rode through the traffic, I could hear him singing and whistling to himself. As we were making our way back towards where I was staying, I half turned in my seat and asked, "So where is a good place to get beer?"

Out of the corner of my eye I could see his face light up as he asked,

"I take you where I go?"

The idea of a local bar sounded like a good one, and sure beat the idea of going back to my hot, stuffy, depressing room.

"OK. Let's go and I will buy you a beer. Is the beer cold?"

I added the last question more out of conversation than anything else, and initially, did not think anything further of his answer,

"Yes, I think they have ice."

A couple of minutes later we pulled up outside what appeared to be a mechanic's garage. The driver hopped off the cyclo and I followed him inside. The garage had been cleared out, leaving just an oil-smeared concrete floor. As we entered, plastic tables and folding chairs were being set up to create an after-hours pub! We took our seats at a table and sat to face the evening traffic passing by the entrance of the shop. For the first time that day, the intensity of the sun began to diminish and dusk started to descend on the city. The bartender came around and offered us a plastic cup each and filled them with beer from a jerry can. The beer was at room temperature.

"Ah, you want cold beer?"

The driver called out to the bartender, who came back and, before I knew what was happening, dropped ice into my beer. I could only hope that the alcohol in the beer would kill any of the bugs in the ice (which was probably made from tap water). Furthermore, the ice only served to water down the beer. Although the beer was still warm as well as being watered down, it was nevertheless relaxing to sit back and watch the world go by.

While we were sitting there, hawkers would pass by trying to sell their wares. Most of it was junk, but one guy was selling small bags of small hardboiled eggs. I bought some, assuming them to be quail eggs or something similar. I offered half of them to the driver who happily accepted them, and for five minutes we were busy peeling and eating the eggs, which with a bit of salt tasted quite nice. After a while I asked him where the eggs were from. Rather than give me the name of a bird species, he answered,

"From bird nest around the city."

I could only assume he meant they were pigeon eggs. I ordered another round of drinks to make sure there was enough alcohol to kill off any pathogenic bacteria from the pigeon eggs (well, it seemed like a good enough reason to me to have another drink).

Once he was onto his second drink, the cyclo driver seemed quite relaxed, so I thought I would ask him for his life story. I started with a simple enough lead-off question.

"Are you from Ho Chi Minh City?"

The driver was originally from a rural village in the south, but had come to the city five or ten years earlier (he hadn't really kept count of the years) to make money to help support his family. When he first came to the city he used to sleep on his cyclo, but after being robbed while he slept and losing all the money he had, he decided to pay a local landlord to allow him to sleep indoors on the floor of a room with other people. He would go back and see his family once or twice a year and give them the money that he earned. He believed it was all worth it because it meant that his children could be educated rather than have to help work the land. I wanted to ask him how old he was, but looking at his deeply tanned, leathery skin he could have been anything from twenty to forty-five. Despite his openness, I suddenly felt rather intrusive asking such personal questions, so instead, ordered another round of drinks.

By now the sun had set and it was dark. Over the third drink we just chatted about fairly superficial subjects. The cyclo driver was now quite tipsy and it was probably best for all concerned that he had no more to drink. I announced to the cyclo driver that I was very tired and was going to go back to where I was staying. Fortunately, I had found out earlier that I was only a five minute walk from there. I paid what seemed a pittance for the drinks, and perhaps out of a feeling guilt for haggling with a man who had so little, paid the cyclo driver the full 100,000 dong. I thanked him for a great afternoon and left.

After tracing my steps back to where I was staying to make sure that I would not get lost, I decided to head down to the nearby Night Market to get something to eat. These markets are held outside the buildings that house the central Ben Tanh Market. Once the Ben Tanh Market closes for the day, the street is closed off and the Night Market opens for business. The market includes a number of food stalls which set up small restaurants on the empty road.

I chose one of these temporary restaurants at random and sat down on a wooden stool at a small wooden table. A waiter came out and thoughtfully offered me a menu in English (I was by now far too tired to try and communicate across the language barrier). Squinting at the menu in the flickering light of a candle, the salt and pepper squid caught my attention, as it was something that I had never tried before.

I placed my order and enjoyed the pleasant evening air as I sipped on my water.

The squid arrived within ten minutes. It had been cut into squares and scored so that when it was cooked it formed little curls. The plate was served with a lime garnish and for the first of many times in Vietnam, I experienced the unique flavor combination of salt, pepper, and lime juice. The squid was hot and fresh and the salt, pepper, and lime flavors tasted amazing. It definitely beat the rubbery fried calamari and tartar sauce I was normally used to.

Eventually I returned to my room. Despite it having cooled down outside, my room was still stiflingly hot. Even with the fan on maximum power and directly angled at my face, I felt uncomfortable. Although I had barely slept in the last forty-eight hours, I lay awake most of that night thinking about the day I had just had: my first day back on the road after so many years.

Already I had learned a couple of useful lessons.

Never believe half the claims made in guidebooks. Especially when it says how easy it is to find a hotel room and that it is just a simple matter of turning up and picking somewhere to stay! At least book your first night. When you are lugging a backpack and are operating on only a few hours of sleep after a long-haul flight, you just want things to be easy. You don't want an adventure. The other thing was to not be cheap when it comes choosing to somewhere to stay. It doesn't matter how cheap a room is, if you are not comfortable and cannot sleep, you are never going to enjoy your travel.

But my most important lesson of the day was a positive one.

Sure, the guidebook is useful for giving you a feel for the things to do in a new city, and its importance in this regard cannot be overstated. But when I left it behind and just walked the streets of the city with my eyes open, I had some amazing experiences. I ate some great food and during the course of a chance meeting with the cyclo driver, got to experience the city from a completely different angle, which even included a small insight into how some of the people lived here.

I really enjoyed the taste of the salt and pepper squid. I was later surprised when I discovered just how easy it was to prepare. It has now become one of my favorite quick dishes and always evokes memories of that day in Vietnam.

The Hungry Traveller's Salt & Pepper Squid – serves 4

Shopping List

450g (1 lb.) Squid rings or pieces
2 tbsp. Coarse salt
1 tbsp. Ground black pepper
½ Cup corn flour
Vegetable oil for frying
2 Halved limes

Preparation

Step 1:
Wash the squid pieces and pat them dry with paper towel.

Step 2:
Combine the salt and pepper with the corn flour.

Step 3:
Toss the squid in the seasoned flour. Make sure that the squid pieces are evenly coated.

Step 4:
Heat the oil in a wok or deep sided fry pan suitable for deep frying. When the oil is hot, cook the squid in batches, until the rings turn golden and are crispy.

Step 5:
Drain the cooked squid on paper towel.

Step 6:
Squeeze over the lime and serve.

My Most Memorable Burger Experience

Location: Meknes, Morocco

I consider myself somewhat of a burger connoisseur. I believe that my teenage years spent flipping burgers is as good a grounding as any to this claim. And to be clear, the basic definition of a hamburger is a broiled ground beef patty IN A BUN. The sheer disappointment I have felt on a number of occasions in Europe when ordering a burger, only to be presented with a broiled meat patty with a side salad, is beyond description. This is followed closely by those trendy eateries that seem to think it is très chic to serve up their burgers in some sort of open sandwich arrangement.

At least the Americans know how to make a hamburger!

During my trips to the USA, I must have munched my way through half a cow's worth of ground beef (and a couple of pig backs – after all, the only thing better than a hamburger is a bacon hamburger with a slice of Monterey Jack cheese – my mouth still waters while my arteries harden at the memory).

Yes, the USA is definitely the home of the best burgers I have eaten. But ask me to name the most memorable experience I have had eating a burger, and my answer is a small food market on the town outskirts of Meknes in Morocco.

It was lunchtime and we were in a crumbling-looking souk in Meknes that sold fresh produce. I was keen to try my first ever camel burger and apparently, this was the place to get them. After forty minutes we had walked around the entire market twice and there was definitely no stall selling camel burgers. There was however, a guy who had a stall which consisted of a large grill on which he had been fervently cooking up food. My first attempt at trying to ask for a burger resulted in a quizzical look. We walked away disheartened at the time, having been so easily defeated by the language barrier.

However, it was clear that this was the only stall in the market that even remotely looked like it could sell a camel burger. I had been assured that I could get camel burgers at this market, so we walked back to the store holder with fresh resolve. I was not going to let my inability to speak Arabic or French get in the way of trying camel.

I decided to watch the stall for a while to see if he was serving up anything that remotely resembled a camel burger. My plan was to rush up and begin to furiously point at the food. I hoped that the man would miraculously interpret this flailing of my arms as meaning *One camel burger please - and no I do not want fries. Thanks.*

Perhaps fortunately for my self-respect, the opportunity did not present itself.

However by watching the stream of people coming to and from the stall, it soon became obvious that he was providing a cooking service. People brought him their fresh ingredients that they had bought in the market and within five minutes he would turn the ingredients into a cooked dish. Unfortunately no one seemed to be requesting him to cook camel burgers, despite the fact that I had been loitering there for around ten minutes.

"My friend, he is a very good cook."

For once on my travels I actually felt pleased to hear the opening patter of the opportunistic huckster.

"Is that a fact?"

I replied, while trying to sound as nonchalant as possible. Inside I was mentally toughening myself up for the haggling that I knew was soon to commence. After all the travel that I had done through North Africa, the Middle East, and Asia, I was still completely inept at bargaining.

"Of course. All the people come here. He is the Jamie Oliver of Morocco!"

I was going to explain why I did not think that comparison was a good selling point, but I was hungry.

"Can he make an excellent camel burger?"

"Camel burger?"

There was a pause, and then,

"Yes, yes of course. You give me the food and I will tell him."

"I don't have the food."

Another pause. It was a little surprising, but this was a smaller town. Maybe the hucksters had less opportunities to sharpen their craft.

"You come with me. I make a good price for you and your friend and I will take care of everything!"

Salvation!

After a few minutes of one-sided negotiations, the price for my salvation was agreed.

For the next twenty minutes, I followed him around the market to make sure he did not run off with my money.

First stop was the butcher for the camel meat. At least I assumed the stall sold camel meat because of what appeared to be skinned camel heads on display.

"Do you want the hump as well?"

"What?"

He pointed to what looked like pure lard. The expression on my face must have betrayed my thoughts.

"Just a little bit for flavor."

Well I guess when in Rome…

And into a hand grinder went the meat and hump fat. Before handing over the ground meat, the butcher added his "secret spices" (which smelled like cumin) to the mix.

Next were the vegetables. To my surprise, instead of an onion and tomato, my new friend picked out an onion, zucchini, and a bell pepper. I guess I could be open-minded! Finally the bakery, where he bought large, round bread rolls. They were still warm to the touch.

And then it was back to "Jamie Oliver." After a few minutes of back and forth and some exaggerated gesticulation between our huckster friend and the cook (who clearly wanted a decent cut of the former's "service fee"), the food was handed over.

And after around five or ten minutes, it was ready. It may have taken us almost two hours to get there, but there it was, a genuine Moroccan-style camel burger: a bread round with a large juicy-looking meat patty stuffed with sautéed onion, zucchini, and bell peppers. We thanked the cook and our go-between and walked around to the side of the shop. Crouching down in the dusty lane we leaned against the wall of the building and took our first bite into the burger.

And the taste?

It was pretty good! The fat of the hump, having melted into the cooked meat, made the burger patty very juicy. The cumin also pretty much masked any distinctive "camel taste" the meat may have had. And although I have never had a burger with sautéed vegetables before, it all went really well together.

I could have eaten another one, but our friend had gone. Clearly he had made enough money out of his thirty minutes of work to take the rest of the afternoon off!

The following is a pretty simple dish, based on the recipe I use for my ever-popular hamburgers that I serve up when I have a barbecue. I have added a twist with the seasonings that I use to recreate the flavors of that burger I had in Meknes. However, you can use ground beef, just in case your local supermarket does not stock ground camel. If you do use camel, don't forget to add the hump fat!

The Hungry Traveller's Homemade
Moroccan Style Hamburger – serves 6

Shopping List

700g (1.5 lbs.) of quality ground beef

2/3 cup of carnation evaporated milk

1 egg

½ cup bread crumbs

1 onion

6 large round bread rolls (or hamburger buns)

1 large zucchini

1 large bell pepper

Salt and cumin to taste

Preparation

Step 1:

Combine the beef, evaporated milk, egg, bread crumbs, salt and cumin in a mixing bowl. Mixing the ingredients by hand tends to give the best results. Form the mixture into 6 patties and refrigerate.

Step 2:

Prepare the vegetables; slice the onion into rings, cut the zucchini into lengthway slices, and Julienne the bell pepper.

Step 3:

Sauté the vegetables.

Step 4:

Barbecue or broil the hamburger patties.

Step 5:

Place the cooked meat patty onto a toasted roll and top with the sautéed vegetables.

Of course, if you prefer a more traditional style of hamburger, instead of seasoning the meat with cumin, use pepper or perhaps mustard. And do not use zucchini and bell peppers (but still keep the sautéed onions!). Add your favorite cheese, and perhaps slices of tomato and iceberg lettuce.

A Step Back in Time

Location: Singapore

Not everything I remember from my travels is centered around food. Sometimes it is drink as well.

I first visited the city-state of Singapore as a tourist, and then later, lived there for a period of time. It is a place of great contrasts: physical, economic, political and social. However as a short-term tourist, the most obvious thing that strikes you are some of the physical contrasts in the city.

For the most part, the downtown of the city appears to be all glass and steel skyscrapers. The city seems to be focused towards the future, with new development, as an increasing number of towers fill in more of the gaps in the city skyline. All of this provides testament to the government's policy of central planning and the direct sponsorship of major economic initiatives since the 1960s.

However, in among this city that is dedicated to the future, are still pockets that point to its past. These include Singapore's old established gardens, such as Fort Canning Park; the old merchant shop houses in the Chinatown district; and the names of different areas, such as Dhoby Ghaut (which roughly translated means "washer men beside the river"), as well as some of the city's surviving colonial era landmark buildings.

Arguably, chief among these is the Raffles Hotel. Named after Sir Stamford Raffles, who established the city, the hotel conjures up images of Singapore's frontiersman past. The modern city was created during the early nineteenth century to capitalize on its location near the Straits of Malacca as well as to support British trade between China and India.

For me, it represents a romanticized past age consisting of rogue Victorian era fortune-seekers, wearing khaki safari suits and pith helmets, at a time of the zenith of British influence. The hotel itself is the stuff of legend, having hosted both Joseph Conrad and Rudyard Kipling, whose works captured the spirit of this time. The fact that the last tiger in Singapore was pursued into and shot in the hotel, further adds to this frontier town image that is so completely at odds with the modern Singapore.

However, what the hotel is also famous for is its *Long Bar* and its famous cocktail, the Singapore Sling. The bar is also famous for having wooden boxes of unshelled peanuts on every table; the protocol is for patrons to discard the peanut shells directly onto the floor.

As a result of all this, I had an image of a slightly faded, turn of the twentieth century bar with dishevelled expats in crushed linen suits slumped in silence over their Singapore Slings. The only noise, I imagined, would be the *swoop swoop* of a slow-moving electric fan and the occasional *crunch crunch* as years of discarded peanut shells were steadily crushed into dust while the barman moved around collecting empty glasses.

Armed with this image, I approached the Raffles Hotel. As a low rise building near a busy traffic intersection, it seemed slightly out of place in such modern surroundings. To the side of the whitewashed hotel building, were the outside stairs that led up to the second-floor entrance to the Long Bar. So far, so good. I then walked along the balcony corridor and entered the world famous Long Bar.

My first impressions did not disappoint me. It was mid-afternoon and quite empty. I was surrounded by dark wood and brass in the bar area, with the rest of the room consisting of tables with wicker chairs. I took a seat and saw the spiral wooden staircase leading to the upper level. I looked up and saw exposed wooden beams on which were mounted a series of large mechanical swinging fans. However, the purpose of the fans was not to provide much needed cooling relief to the patrons; like all buildings in Singapore, the Long Bar is air-conditioned.

But this was only the beginning of the shattering of my romanticized image of the Long Bar. Looking across to the bar I noticed for the first time, a series of modern *Tiger Beer* taps mounted at regular intervals.

There were unshelled peanuts on the table but the floor was in pristine condition – hardly encouraging me to start littering it with my own used shells. Despite this, I did throw some shells on the floor, but immediately felt like a guilty child for making a mess. The disapproving looks I got from what appeared to be another group of tourists at a nearby table did not help the situation.

Yet greater disappointment was still to come.

I placed my order for a Singapore Sling at the bar. Given

the extortionate price for the drink (even by Singapore standards, where alcohol already tends to be very expensive), I was expecting the barman to produce a cocktail shaker and start mixing my drink. Instead, he poured it out of a bottle of pre-mix.

I sat down at my table. By now my image of the Long Bar was completely crushed. I now knew beyond any shadow of a doubt, that there would *never* have been a time when this establishment served up Singapore Slings to a line of dishevelled expats who, propping up the main bar, spent their time drinking away the pain of their washed up dreams of fortune.

Why?

Because the Singapore Sling is *bright pink* in color!

Of course, if I had taken the time to read the history of the drink that was at the table, I would have learned that it was designed to be a woman's drink. Yet I am a New Age Man and could have looked past the color. However, the sickly sweet taste meant that drinking a Singapore Sling in the Long Bar of the Raffles Hotel would always be a once in a lifetime experience for me!

It turned out, however, that this would not be my last visit to the Long Bar. Later on, waves of overseas visitors would come to visit me and insist on having a genuine Singapore Sling at the Long Bar. I would sip on a cold Tiger Beer and smile at the almost universal reaction to the "Singapore Sling Experience." I would then take my visitors out to the bars that were far more reflective of the bold, vibrant city that is Singapore.

The following is the recipe for a Singapore Sling. I would like to have had a great story of how I was able to covertly lift the recipe while the head barman was not looking, but the reality is that the recipe is displayed in the Long Bar for all to see.

The Hungry Traveller's Original Singapore Sling – serves 1

Shopping List

30 mL (1 oz.) gin
15 mL (½ oz.) cherry brandy
120 mL (4 oz.) pineapple juice
15 mL (½ oz.) lime juice
7.5 mL (¼ oz.) Cointreau
7.5 mL (¼ oz.) Dom Benedictine
10 mL (1/3 oz.) Grenadine
Dash of Angostura Bitters
Pineapple Slice and Maraschino cherry

Preparation

Step 1:
Pour all of the liquid ingredients into a cocktail shaker with ice.

Step 2:
Strain and pour into a Collins glass. There should be a pale pink foam on the top of the drink.

Step 3:
Garnish with the pineapple slice and Maraschino cherry.

La Dolce Vita

Location: Rome, Italy

I am always amazed at how accessible it is to see the grandeur that was Ancient Rome. The Roman Forum, the Palatine Hill, and the Colosseum are all within relatively easy walking distance of each other. The size and scale of the site is quite humbling, and it is easy to appreciate the cliché of Rome being an enormous outdoor museum.

However, as I walked through the ruins of the Forum, I felt saddened by how little of that grandeur still remained. The ancient monuments so accessible to people today were even more accessible over the last 1,500 years, during which they were cannibalized as a free source of building materials, especially travertine.

In fact, some of the buildings in the area of the Forum, such as the Basilica Julia, were already in ruins by late antiquity, having already been stripped of all reusable material. This once enormous multi story building, with a floor area about the size of a football field, now consists of no more than its podium, a few blocks on which statues once stood, and parts of the brick walls.

However, don't get me wrong: what remains of the Forum is dramatic, and it is still possible to get a sense of the real drama of what once was the civic and legal center of the Roman Empire. There are the three remaining enormous columns rising from the ruins of the Temple of Castor and Pollux and the Arch of Septimius Severus. Or perhaps, for those with a keen sense of history, there is the low brown wall next to the arch, the Rostra. It is here that Mark Antony most likely delivered his legendary eulogy after the assassination of Julius Caesar – but not the words immortalized by Shakespeare of "Friends, Romans, countrymen, lend me your ears." According to Plutarch, in what appears to be a no less impassioned speech, Mark Antony grabbed the clothes of Caesar and, showing the bloody stab wounds, denounced the assassins. This speech, combined with the reading out of Caesar's will, in which most of his property was left to the people of Rome, was pivotal in turning popular opinion against the conspirators.

Thus, with a sense of history and a bit of imagination it is possible to appreciate the importance of this site to European history.

However, that yearning to see at least one ancient building in all its original magnificence is still not satisfied.

Granted, there is the Colosseum, whose sheer size has meant that its form has been able to survive the ravages of almost 2,000 years and still look visually impressive enough to dominate the city. Yet it is still a mere shell of its former magnificence, having suffered from earthquakes, fires, and a steady cannibalization of its supply of travertine blocks which, no doubt, were recycled into some of the magnificent buildings of the Renaissance and later periods.

Within the Forum, there is also the Curia, which once

housed the Roman Senate. The brick core of this building has survived because it was consecrated as a church. However, the once magnificent, external marble and stucco cladding that once adorned the building were removed centuries ago.

Arguably, the best example of a building that gives a true sense of the Roman Empire's awe-inspiring architecture is the Pantheon. This is the most complete ancient Roman structure in the city.

I remember the first time that I approached the Pantheon was via a narrow lane. Typical of so many of the most amazing sights in Rome, I turned a corner and the unassuming alley dramatically opened up onto a square called the Piazza della Rotonda, with the imposing form of the Pantheon right in front of me!

I don't remember what I was struck by more: the enormous columns supporting the pediment that formed the portico of the building; or the actual scale of the pediment itself, emblazoned with its Latin inscription to Agrippa (who built the original temple on this site); or the huge dome that rose up behind the portico in a series of stacked concrete rings, with each successive ring thinner and lighter than the one below it.

The building that we see today was constructed during the reign of Hadrian in around AD 125, to replace the original temple that had been destroyed by fire. Like the Curia, the Pantheon owes its survival to the fact that it was later consecrated as a Christian church, thus avoiding the indignity of being stripped for building materials.

Although the heavily built, masculine appearance of the exterior of the building is imposing enough, it was the contrasting magnificence of the interior that made me feel completely awestruck. No doubt the decor has been remodeled since the original construction, but the marble-clad interior seemed at least sympathetic to a building from Ancient Rome.

However, what amazed me most was how delicate the building appeared on the inside.

The interior of the Pantheon is a huge, round, cavernous space; my eyes were immediately drawn upward towards the heavens and the enormous domed roof that floated above me with no visible supporting columns or vaulting. However, what I loved most about the structure was that rather than the dome being closed off to the sky, an oculus at the dome's apex had been left open to allow light (and all the other elements, including rain) into the building.

The roof of the building, more than anything else, gave me that sense of the grandeur of Ancient Rome that I had failed to instinctively feel when wondering around the Forum. Even so, the Forum and the other crumbling ancient sites seem to hold the "ghosts" and the sense of history that I felt the Pantheon may have lacked.

What also struck me about the Pantheon was that the architectural and engineering skills used to construct this building were so sophisticated, that after the fall of Rome, it would be well over a 1,000 years before the next monumentally sized dome would be attempted in Western Europe, with Michelangelo's design for the dome of St Peter's Basilica.

After visiting the Pantheon I sat at an outdoor table at one of the cafes on the Piazza della Rotonda to admire the

Pantheon and enjoy the spring sunshine. Given that it was still relatively early in the morning, I ordered a cappuccino. As I sat back enjoying the moment, sipping my coffee, feeling the sun on my face, and admiring a piece of Ancient Rome that was still alive and well, I saw two buskers preparing to perform in the Piazza. Oh well, I thought, I guess all good things have to come to an end.

However, when the busking pair, a man and a woman, started singing opera (I have no idea which one it was), I ended up enjoying my most perfect Italian experience.

It was the perfect embodiment of Rome being the "eternal city" meant to me. Over the centuries Rome has seen the rise and fall of kings, consuls, emperors, Popes and dictators. Yet the city itself has been the continuous thread linking all of these events together. And in that Piazza, whose cobbles were probably laid down around 500 years ago, I admired a building that has stood and survived some 2,000 years of political, economic, and social changes, listening to an opera that was probably first performed a bit over 100 years ago, while sipping on a style of coffee that is synonymous with Italy and had that been made within the last ten minutes.

I sat back, closed my eyes and thought, this is La Dolce Vita!

The following recipe is for making a cappuccino – and yes, to do this at home, you will require a steam producing espresso machine. You will not however, need the industrial-sized machines that you see in coffee shops. There are a number of domestic coffeemakers available with a boiler and steam arm for heating and frothing milk.

The cappuccino was first patented in Milan at the turn of the twentieth century and developed into its current form by the 1950s, with the introduction of the high-pressure espresso machine.

The best cappuccino should be one-third espresso, one-third milk and one-third froth, with powdered chocolate sprinkled on the top.

The Hungry Traveller's Perfect Cappuccino – serves 1

Shopping List

An espresso maker
A coffee cup
A wide bottomed jug
Water
Fresh, cold milk
Ground coffee

Preparation

Step 1: Heat the water

Different espresso machines will vary. However, make sure there is enough water in the tank of the machine so that the pump pipes are fully submerged. Turn on the power and pump water into the boiler. Turn on the boiler to heat the water. The handle that holds the coffee is called the group handle, which should be locked into the machine. Once the water is at the correct temperature (there should be some sort of light on the machine to indicate this), turn off the boiler and press the dosage button and allow water to flow through the handle for about 10 seconds to both clean it and heat it to the same temperature as the water.

Step 2: Add the coffee

For a single shot of espresso you will need one spoonful of coffee. Place the coffee in the filter basket and tap it to create a level surface. Compact the coffee. This will ensure that the water doesn't flow through it too quickly.

Step 3: Filter

Lock the group handle into the machine and put a coffee cup underneath. Turn on the dosage button. The coffee should take 14 to 18 seconds to filter through for a single espresso and 20 to 25 seconds for a double.

Step 4: Steam the milk

This requires using the steam arm on the coffee machine. To produce the frothy milk, insert the arm into a jug of milk so that the tip is just below the surface. Turn the steam arm on and froth the milk.

Step 5: Add the milk

Swirl the milk around to create a dense, smooth foam. Using a large spoon to hold back the froth, pour the warmed milk into the cup (approximately one third of the cup volume). Top up the cup with the froth (you may need to use a spoon to make sure the froth comes out). Sprinkle drinking chocolate over the surface. Enjoy!

The World's Best Kebab
(well, at least in my opinion)

Location: Melbourne, Australia

And now for something really controversial: Where is the world's best kebab?

Wherever there is a large Greek, Turkish, or Lebanese community in the world, there will most likely be a kebab shop. They might go by different names such as gyros, souvlakia, doner, or sharwarma, but essentially it is almost universally the same thing: thin slices of meat cut from a huge rotating spit, with salad and sauce, crammed into some sort of bread to create the ultimate fast food. The success of the kebab can be seen by the fact that it is eaten widely throughout the world – and although often written off in western countries as a fast track to food poisoning, due to the dodgy kebabs that are sold from kebab vans in the early hours of the morning to unsuspecting victims as they roll out of bars and clubs, when cooked with care and fresh ingredients it can be the "food of the gods!"

And before you flood my publisher with letters of complaint, I know that there are a multitude of different ethnic groups that have a similar food concept, and that there are a ton of variations as to what could be defined as a kebab – but this is *my* story based on *my* experiences!

So what are the criteria I use for judging a good kebab?

Is it actually a kebab?

It must actually meet my basic definition of a kebab. It must consist of pieces of meat cut from a large rotating skewer with sauce and salad, wrapped in some sort of bread. It definitely cannot be what I call a deconstructed kebab, my term for the meat, salad and sauce served on a dish. You must be able to eat a kebab with your fingers!

Meat

It must be lamb or chicken. Sorry, but no pork. I have also heard of places that try to pass off fish as a meat filling in a kebab – this definitely does not qualify!

Sauce

A good kebab shop should have a homemade sauce. As a result, I am quite open to the type of sauce, provided that it goes with the kebab (which a good homemade sauce should do). Anything that comes out of a bottle labeled Heinz does not qualify!

Salad

This is really subjective, and I have had many different options that all tasted good, from the simple lettuce, tomato, and red onion; to red cabbage; to tabouleh; to cooked potatoes. Therefore the main requirement is for the salad filling to be fresh and to go with the other flavors in the kebab.

Bread

This is important to me. Whether it is pita, a wrap, or a round bread roll, I am open to many different options, provided that the bread is fresh and served warm.

Overall presentation

A kebab is finger food. It should be well filled but not overly so; the filling and sauce should not fall out all over the place when you try to eat it. It should also be packaged and served so that it is food that you can eat while on the move.

Sides

Typical sides of fries and dips are not used directly to judge the kebab, but the quality of the sides that you can get, do tend to be representative of the quality of the kebab.

So who are on my short list of contenders?

Kebab shop near Grand Bazaar entrance: Istanbul, Turkey

Anyone who has been to the Grand Bazaar will realize that the directions I have given to finding this place are as good as useless, given the large number of entrances into the Grand Bazaar!

The shop operates out of a window onto the main street. Although there are probably countless places like this in Turkey, it was memorable because for not a lot of money, you could get a fresh bread roll full of kebab meat and potatoes covered in the meat juices that had run off the kebab as it cooked.

It was simple. It was cheap. And it was tasty.

Street side kebab stall: Fira (Santorini), Greece

Fira, the main town in Santorini, is essentially a one street town. On the main street, just up from the bus terminus, is a street stall where for a couple of euros you can buy a gyros and a Mythos beer. Apart from the obvious attractions of having a cold beer on a hot summer day, the gyros, although small in size, was extremely tasty. In my opinion this was because the meat cooked on the spit was well caramelized, and because the kebab was also packed with fries seasoned with paprika.

Unfortunately, there are very few seats outside the stall, so quite often you will be eating your food while sitting on the nearby steps or by the adjacent roadside gutter. During the day this can be quite undignified when people try to step over you. However, late at night, after being out at the clubs and bars, people tend to be a little less self-conscious about sitting in the gutter at 2:00 a.m., and are far more focused on eating their food.

However, the fact that the kebab is not served rolled in paper means that you are dependent on using your paper plate to avoid the contents falling all over the ground (or worse still, all over you) and being turned into a stinking, garlicky mess.

Afghan Food Stall in Vic Market Place Food Court: Melbourne, Australia

This food court is attached to the Queen Victoria Markets in Melbourne, Australia.

As far as markets go, Queen Victoria Markets has something for everyone. Tourists are drawn to the general item stalls, where it is possible to buy cheaper souvenirs, but what I was really impressed by was the food market – not just the fresh fruit, vegetables, meat, and fish that you would generally expect to find in such a market, but also the shops selling small goods, specialty cakes and biscuits, and other products that you would expect to find in a continental deli.

Apart from the food market, there is also a food court. I found the food court by accident and noticed an Afghan food stall. Out of curiosity, I looked at what they had to sell, and saw that they had Afghan-style kebabs. To be honest, I have no idea how authentic the kebab was. To me it seemed all pretty standard: slices of lamb, garlic yogurt sauce, and salad. However, it was wrapped in an enormous piece of warm, traditional Afghan bread, which is considerably thicker than regular pita bread. And although extremely filling, the thicker bread absorbed all the juices of the meat and the sauce, which is what made the kebab stand out for me.

Stalactites: Melbourne, Australia

This kebab shop is located in the traditional Greek district of central Melbourne. Although it is a strange name for a kebab shop, it does make sense when you sit down and look at the walls and ceiling, which have been decorated to look like the interior of a cave. I won't pretend: it does look tacky and, although it has been around for so long that I am sure there are those who would now label it is kitsch (although I have heard rumors that the restaurant section has been renovated and that the cave decorations have been painted over).

Stalactites is something of an institution in Melbourne, having been in business for over thirty years, and open 24 hours a day, 7 days a week.

Given its proximity to the central Melbourne nightclubs, it is a great place for a kebab at 3:00 a.m. But the food is also quite special because the meat is cooked over charcoal.

Sober, inebriated, or somewhere in between, the food always tastes fantastic.

South Meze: London, United Kingdom (before the change of owners)

For a few years this was my local kebab shop. It was owned and staffed by three Turkish guys: the owner, the waiter/delivery guy, and "Chef." Despite being a suburban restaurant, every Wednesday they would take delivery of vast quantities of shoulder of lamb, which they would then grind up and season on-site before pressing it around the huge skewers that would form the rotating vertical spit, on which they would cook the meat during the following week.

It was at this kebab shop where I first tried red cabbage in a kebab.

But what I loved most about the kebabs at this place was Chef's cooking, and in particular, his homemade chili sauce. As you would expect, the recipe was a secret, but he did tell me that it took him over a day and a half to cook it down, and given the depth of flavor of the sauce, this was easy to believe.

Every Friday I would order a large kebab with red

cabbage and chili sauce and a side of fries covered in chili sauce. When we moved away from the area we would get the food home delivered.

However, the owner eventually sold up the business and Chef moved on. The chili sauce started to taste like something that had been bought from the local supermarket, and the quality of the doner meat deteriorated. Even the red cabbage was so soggy that it made the kebab inedible.

All in all, it was an ignominious end to an establishment that seemingly had the perfect product, which was destroyed by the incompetence of the new owners.

And the winner is?

It has to be Stalactites.

Why? Well in simple terms it checks all of the boxes on my list. The kebabs also taste great and it seems that just about everyone who has eaten a kebab from Stalactites has enjoyed their food. And besides, there is something about a place where you can buy a kebab for breakfast – not something that I have ever done, but it is always good to know that it is there if you want it!

Unless you have a spit over an open charcoal fire it is very difficult to create the flavors of an authentic kebab. However, the following chicken recipe does maximize the flavor of the meat fairly well by poaching it in stock before frying the meat until it caramelizes. It is a process that requires a bit of trial and error to perfect, but it does allow you to make a chicken kebab at home!

The Hungry Traveller's Homemade Chicken Kebab – serves 4

Shopping List
700g (1.5 lbs.) of roughly diced chicken breast or thighs (I prefer to remove the skin)

Tzatziki or similar garlic and yogurt sauce

Chicken stock

Olive oil

4 large pita bread (or any similar flat bread suitable for use as a wrap)

Your favorite salad fillings (I like lettuce, red onion and tomato)

Preparation
Step 1:

Poach the chicken in as small a volume of chicken stock as possible. Once the chicken is cooked, roughly shred the chicken with two forks.

Step 2:

Turn up the heat on the fry pan to allow the remaining liquid stock to boil away (alternatively the stock can be discarded and you can move onto the next step, but a lot of flavor will be lost).

Step 3:

Once the liquid has gone, put aside the chicken. Put a little cooking oil in the fry pan and return it to a high heat. Once the fry pan is hot, fry off the chicken until it starts to brown. Once the chicken has caramelized, take it off the heat.

Step 4:

Heat the pita bread in a fry pan over medium heat, constantly turning the bread over to avoid burning it. Ensure that the bread is served piping hot.

Step 5:

Assemble the kebab by spooning on the Tzatziki, adding the chicken and then the salad filling.

Step 6:

Tightly roll the pita to form the kebab. For an authentic experience, wrap the kebab in foil to help. This will hold it together and make it easier to eat with your fingers!

Drunken Prawns

Location: Da Lat, Vietnam

After two weeks of traveling around the southern regions of Vietnam in close to 100 degrees heat and seemingly 100 per cent humidity, the town of Da Lat provided welcome relief. Perched in the central highlands of Vietnam, Da Lat's temperate climate was in sharp contrast to the prevailing tropical climate that I had been experiencing at sea level.

The town was established as a resort center at the beginning of the twentieth century, during the era of French colonial rule. It was built around a large artificial lake, and with its architecture, pine trees, orchards, and climate, is reminiscent of a European village.

Da Lat's reputation as a honeymooners' destination held little appeal to me, as I was traveling solo at the time. After visiting the two major attractions of the area: the Art Deco Summer Palace (which belonged to Bao Dai, the last Vietnamese emperor) and the Hang Nga guesthouse (also known as the "crazy house"), I found myself with half a day to fill in.

As a result I decided to walk around the perimeter of the lake. I wandered along the winding road from my guesthouse down to the lake and began my walk. After about thirty or forty minutes I had reached the far side and was enjoying the quiet. I was also enjoying, for the first time since arriving in Vietnam, the experience of walking around for so long without being completely bathed in perspiration.

Then, about fifty yards ahead of me, on the grass verge between the path and the edge of the lake, I saw a group of four men who, if not drunk, were well on the way to getting there. As I approached, one of them called out,

"Ha-looo!"

To which ensued a drunken chorus of

"Ha-looo! Ha-looo! Ha-looooooooooooooooo!" and riotous laughter broke out.

I was not going to be put off by what appeared to be a gathering of the local yokels (after all, I had learned all the common Vietnamese phrases in the back of my guidebook), and I replied to their greeting,

"Xin chao."

This prompted some laughter and a discussion among the men before one of them replied in broken English,

"You, come" and motioned to a patch of ground next to him.

Disregarding all of the advice that has ever been given about trusting strangers, I sat down.

I then spied the source of the men's merriment, a plastic jerry can half-full of home-brewed beer. No doubt it had started the day completely full. One of the men offered me a drink. Sensing my hesitation, he took a swig and again motioned me to drink. The other men looked at me expectantly. I was feeling thirsty and took a long drink, being careful not to end up bathing in the two gallons or so of beer that was swooshing back and forth in the container. For warm beer, it was surprisingly OK. I finished drinking, looked around at their smiles and approving nods, and handed back the jerry can, saying "Cam on" as thanks to my hosts.

"You speak Vietnam?"

I shook my head, to the disappointment of my new friends.

We then engaged in a sequence of small talk, communicating through broken English, a smattering of Vietnamese, and a lot of gesticulation.

One of the men pointed at himself and motioned around him and said "Da Lat" before pointing at me. I replied "Uc" and they nodded and grinned. I then grabbed my stomach and squeezed out an "Uc" as if I had been punched. It was a cheesy joke but always seemed to get a positive response, and this time was no exception. On the other hand, these guys were so stewed they would have laughed at anything, and they spent the next five or ten minutes grabbing their stomachs and groaning "Uc," "Uc," "Uc."

I then endured the other usual questions and conversation pieces that I had experienced many times over the last two weeks.

One of the men rubbed his cheeks and pointed at me. I hadn't shaved in almost a week and had a half-decent beard growing. I unbuttoned the top button of my shirt to show off the top of my chest hair, and one of the guys pulled on it to see if it was real. I was quite shocked: I was used to the kids who were hawking things in the streets being fascinated and calling me "hairy ape man," but to see adult men behaving like this was something I had not expected.

This form of communication continued for a while. Most of the conversation consisted of blue bar humor communicated through universal gestures. These guys were definitely the yokel population of Da Lat.

Then one of the men produced a small butane stove and a dirty old deep-walled fry pan from a bag. Another produced a bag of small, green prawns. Once the burner had been lit and the pan was hot, the man who could speak some broken English emptied in the bag of prawns and started stirring them with a pair of dirty chopsticks. He then grabbed the jerry can and began to pour in some beer. At this point one of his drinking buddies thought it would be funny to give him a hand, and tilted up the container.

The resultant tidal wave of beer almost washed the prawns out of the pan, much to the initial consternation of the cook and the hilarity of his companions. After a brief interaction with the joker of the group, my friend the cook also broke into hysterics. Seeing my confused look, he attempted to explain,

"OK. OK. Drunk prawns. Drunk prawns. Good, good. Good, good."

After another five or ten minutes of letting the prawns boil away, the heat was turned off. The resultant mess did not look appetizing, but as if on cue, my drinking friends all produced chopsticks and tucked into the food, peeling off the shells to devour the meat while sucking on and savoring the heads.

Soon the moment I had been dreading occurred: they motioned for me to try the food! I pulled out my pocket knife and peered into the pot of dirty froth interspersed with prawn and shell fragments. I smiled, teeth gritted, and stabbed at the most edible looking prawn; then I peeled off the shell, closed my eyes, and popped it into my mouth.

I would like to say that what happened next was one of the most unexpected taste sensations of my life. But it tasted exactly as I had expected: an overcooked, chewy, gritty piece of prawn meat with a boiled beer sauce. At least it was probably boiled long enough to minimize the risk of food poisoning.

At this point, I left my new found drinking friends to finish off their food and the still considerable, quantity of beer.

Clearly, what was cooked that afternoon on the shores of Lake Xuan Huong was not the classic recipe for Drunken Prawns. In fact, it was not until several years later that I even realized that Drunken Prawns was a Chinese dish, when I ordered it out of curiosity in a restaurant in London.

However, each time I see Drunken Prawns on a menu, I think of that afternoon with the yokels of Da Lat and it always brings a wry smile to my face.

The following is one of many recipes for Drunken Prawns. This recipe is for a "dry" version of the dish. The common element of all Drunken Prawn recipes is that the first step consists of placing the prawns in a Chinese wine marinade. Traditionally, the prawns are placed into the wine while still alive. Apparently this produces a better flavor, but personally, I feel more comfortable starting with prawns that have already "expired!"

The Hungry Traveller's Drunken Prawns – serves 2

Shopping List

10 green (uncooked) tiger prawns or king prawns
3 tbsp. of Chinese wine
3 spring onion stalks
3 to 5 slices of fresh ginger
Coriander

Preparation

Step 1:

Shell and de-vein the prawns (be sure to leave on the heads and tails).

Step 2:

Place the prawns in a dish and pour 2 tbsp. of the Chinese wine over the prawns. Set to one side for at least 10 minutes to marinade.

Step 3:

Arrange the prawns in a single layer in a steamer. Pour over the marinating wine.

Step 4:

Place the spring onion stalks and ginger on top of the prawns. Drizzle a further 1 tbsp. of Chinese wine over the ingredients.

Step 5:

Steam until the prawns turn completely red. This will only take a few minutes and be sure to not overcook them.

Step 6:

Garnish with coriander and serve.

Oh, I Do Like to be Beside the Seaside

Location: Brighton, England

My first visit to Brighton was everything that I had imagined the English seaside to be. Despite it being July and approaching the peak of summer I was dressed for a wintery day, in long pants and a jacket. The combination of the gray sky, drizzling rain, and the extremely blustery conditions, as well as the fact that it was a weekday, made the seafront look rather forlorn and desolate. Down on the beach, the solitary form of a lifeguard huddled in his shelter was the only object that broke up the landscape of large, palm-sized pebbles.

I started to question whether my extortionate train fare for the day trip down from London had been worthwhile.

Undeterred, however, I pushed on with the day's planned activities, and went into a fish and chip shop near the pier.

"Fish and chips please."

I said, as brightly as possible. After all, if I was going to be down by the English seaside, I should indulge in some traditional food.

"Would you like mushy peas with that?"

"No, thank you." I politely replied.

But inside I was thinking, *eeew*. I knew that mushy peas were a traditional accompaniment to fish and chips, but tradition was not enough to convince me to pay good money to try the gray-green slop that I had seen being served to other customers.

"A pickled onion, perhaps?"

I squinted at the large jar full of white onions in brown vinegar

"OK, I guess."

"How about some bread and butter?"

"What? Why?" I blurted out. This was a tradition I had not heard of before

"I guess that is a *no* then?"

"Sorry. Yes. I mean no thanks."

"Eating in or take away?"

"Take away please"

"There is no additional charge for eating in."

The woman serving me was looking at me as if I were not quite right in the head. However, whatever the weather, I had a plan and I was sticking to it.

My order was wrapped in white paper and handed across to me. It was already covered in large, translucent splotches due to the oil and grease soaking through the paper.

I took my food and headed for the pier. At least it had stopped raining.

Although it was the third pier to be constructed in Brighton, The Brighton Marine Palace and Pier is the only seaside entertainment pier left that is still accessible to the public. Opened at the end of the nineteenth century, in its heyday, the public would pay an admission fee to walk along the pier. At the end of the pier there was a pavilion which was initially used as a concert hall and later, as a theater, as well as a landing stage for boats.

Sadly though, the pier is no longer quite as grand as it once was.

Although it is now free to walk along the length of the pier, I noticed that a lot of the buildings along it have been given over to gaming and slot machines as the pier was purchased by a gaming company during the 1980s.

I have to admit that I was initially quick to judge and dismiss "what the pier had become." But then, looking out westwards, I could see the twisted steel girders and skeletal remains of what had once been the West Pier. The once grand West Pier had gradually slid into a state of terminal decline, a victim of the trend in British vactioners increasingly turning away from native seaside resorts in preference to other European destinations, with its more reliable summer weather. In 1975 the pier was closed to the public due to safety concerns. Then, between 2002 and 2004, the pier and its structures were effectively destroyed by storms and fires.

Looking at what could have easily become of the pier that I was standing on, I realized that it would have been far worse if Brighton had ended up with no pier at all. It was all too easy to decry the tacky glitz of the gaming arcades and miss the fact that this was, overall, a small price to pay for being able to keep the pier. After all, the structure does provide an amazing view back across Brighton's boardwalk; it is free to the public; and there is a series of small food retailers and a small fairground operating at the far end of the pier.

However, I was annoyed to discover during my walk along the pier that it also had a fish and chip restaurant. By now, the white paper packaging holding my lunch was a greasy, soggy mess. Although it was starting to drizzle again, I stopped about halfway along the pier, where one of the amusement arcades acted as a partial windbreak, and opened up my food on the railing of the pier, so that I could complete my plan of eating fish and chips on Brighton Pier. It seemed like such a good idea in theory – and I am sure that on a sunny day it would have been. But the weather was miserable, my fish and chips were soggy, and my pickled onion had fallen out, bounced once on the deck, and plopped into the sea.

Yet my misery was not complete. A flock of hungry seagulls had spotted my food.

If this had been happening to someone else, I no doubt would have laughed.

Around ten seagulls hovered, literally only feet away from me, their bodies suspended in the air as the stiff breeze provided them with all the lift they needed to just hang there. In an attempt to disperse this unwanted gathering, I tore off the batter from my fish (which was quite thick, doughy, and pretty much inedible) and tossed it into the sea. For a few minutes there was a swarming feeding frenzy in the sea below me. Then immediately after, there were three times more birds hovering in front of me.

I began to eat my food, trying to ignore the shrieking birds, and looking at the view back towards the Brighton seafront.

Suddenly the gulls began to swoop, trying to take the food from my hand as I ate it! I felt like I was trapped in that famous scene from Alfred Hitchcock's *The Birds*. As I was about to eat a piece of fish, one of the birds finally succeeded in timing its swoop to perfection, and literally snatched the food from my fingers before I could get it to my mouth. I had finally had enough, and surrendered the rest of my lunch to the seagulls.

As I walked back along the pier, feeling cold, wet, and hunched over against the wind, it was easy to understand why people spend their summer vacations in Spain or the Greek Islands. The outing that I had planned at the quintessential seaside town had pretty much been a disaster.

However, I would keep coming back to visit Brighton.

Just like the wealthy Georgians, who built their summer residences and transformed Brighton from a fishing village into a fashionable resort town during the eighteenth century, people visit Brighton because it is a vibrant town. Being within commuting distance of London makes it is easily accessible to people who want to escape from the city for a day, breathe in the sea air and be reminded of what the sea looks like.

Of course travel was far more difficult back in the time of the Georgians, so they built homes that they could stay in for the summer. The most famous patron of the era was the Prince Regent himself (later King George IV), who constructed his Royal Pavilion in stages between 1787 and 1823. The design of this building sharply contrasts with the traditional Georgian terraces that dominate the architecture of the town. Every time I go to Brighton, I always take time to visit this unusual building, with its fairy tale design consisting of minarets, domes, and towers, which reflected the Georgian fascination with the exoticism of "The East."

And most importantly for me, there are some great places to eat in Brighton, with an almost inexhaustible number of options in *The Lanes* area which is tucked just behind the main boardwalk area.

As you may have gathered, I personally find traditional beer-battered fish and chips a bit heavy to eat; I generally end up peeling off and discarding the thick batter. Therefore my following recipe will no doubt provoke the ire of the traditionalists. The fish is fried in a lighter, tempura-style batter. The chips are also a healthier, oven-baked version, rather than being deep fried, and there are no mushy peas or pickled onions!

The Hungry Traveller's Not So Traditional Fish and Chips – serves 4

Shopping List

Around 700g (1.5 lbs.) of Maris Piper or King Edward potatoes

Olive oil

Around 700g (1.5 lbs.) of hake or cod fillet (although most white fish will be suitable), cut into 4 equal-size pieces

½ cup self-raising flour (plus extra flour for dusting the fish)

½ cup corn flour
1 egg white
1 cup ice-cold sparkling water
Sunflower oil (for frying)

Preparation

The Chips:

Step 1:
Cut the potatoes into even sized wedges or chips and par boil.

Step 2:
Carefully drain. Tip the potatoes onto a clean tea towel and pat them dry. Allow them to cool.

Step 3:
Heat 1 tbsp. of olive oil in a large non-stick roasting tray in an oven on medium-high heat for around 10 minutes.

Step 4:
Toss the cooled par boiled potato wedges/chips with 1 to 2 tbsp. of olive oil in a bowl until all the potatoes are coated with oil.

Step 5:
Tip the potatoes onto the hot roasting pan and arrange the chips so they form a single layer in the pan.

Step 6:
Bake the chips for around 20 to 30 minutes. Turn the chips every 5 to 10 minutes to ensure they crisp on both sides.

The Fish:

Step 1:

Pour the sunflower oil into a fryer or a heavy, deep sided fry pan. Heat the oil.

Step 2:

Pat the fish fillets dry with paper towel. Dust each fillet with self-raising flour and pat off any excess flour.

Step 3:

Mix the self-raising flour, corn flour, a pinch of salt and some pepper in a bowl. Gently pour the sparkling water into the flour mixture and briefly whisk the ingredients. In a separate bowl lightly whisk the egg white until it is frothy and bubbly. Add the whisked egg white to the other batter ingredients and lightly whisk to just mix the ingredients. Avoid over mixing and try and keep as many bubbles in the mixture as possible. This will result in a lighter batter.

Step 4:

To cook the fish; dip the fillet in the batter, let the excess drip off, and then lower it into the hot oil. Fry for 5 to 6 minutes. The cooked fish should be golden all over. Ensure that the oil is hot, before cooking the other pieces of fish.

Recommended Accompaniments

Tartar sauce and a wedge of lemon always goes well with fish and chips!

The Spice Island

Location: Zanzibar, Tanzania

There are places in the world whose very names evoke a sense of the exotic, such as, Kathmandu, Timbuktu, and Zanzibar. Of this list I have managed to visit Zanzibar, and was fortunate enough to do so back in the days before it became fully accessible to mass tourism.

Zanzibar lies off the coast of Tanzania in east Africa. Its location in the Indian Ocean, has given it strategic importance, lying as it does on the trade routes between the Middle East, India, and Africa. The island has at different times been under Persian, Portuguese, Arab, and British influence, until gaining independence in the 1960s.

For me there was always something strangely exotic about Zanzibar. I remember first hearing the name when it was mentioned in the tales of One Thousand and One Nights; a place with a fairy tale name full of magic, Sultans, and princesses. When I was told it was a real place and that it was also known as the Spice Islands, this only increased the sense of intrigue that Zanzibar held for me as a child.

Many years later, and after a slow, rough ferry trip from Dar es Salaam, I remember catching my first sight of Zanzibar and the waterside buildings of the "Stone Town" (also confusingly called "Old Town" by the locals, based on the direct translation of the area's Swahili name of *Mji Mkongwe*). Despite my sea sickness I was not disappointed by what I saw, and that first image will forever be etched in my mind. In the foreground was the glittering blue of the Indian Ocean, leading to the tree-lined boardwalk with the soft light of the afternoon sunshine reflecting off the magnificent yet faded grand buildings of the Sultan's Palace, House of Wonders, and St Joseph's Cathedral.

After docking, and no doubt to demonstrate that Zanzibar is a semi-autonomous part of Tanzania with its own government, we were, rather perversely, made to go through immigration and passport control, despite having caught the ferry from mainland Tanzania.

Once through immigration we were confronted by a wall of aggressive peddlers, each one offering the best, cheapest, and most conveniently located guesthouse in town. Just as well, because I had not arranged any accommodation. I waited for around half an hour, to allow for most of the tourists to be led away by different "handlers," in order to improve the odds of negotiating a decent deal with the ones left behind. After a further fifteen minutes of negotiations, I was able to make arrangements to stay in a guesthouse in the Stone Town.

By the time we checked in it was late afternoon, and we made our way to what had been recommended as the best place to watch the sunset in Stone Town, the Sunset Bar at Africa House. Nowadays Africa House is an upmarket boutique hotel, and the Sunset Bar an upmarket establishment where you can sip cocktails and take in the magnificent views. However, back in the day, the bar was a backpackers' dive, reached by walking up flights of grimy stairs. The decor was faded and worn but well suited to clientele such as me. The bottled beer was disappointingly warm because they had problems with their refrigeration, and could not procure enough ice.

However, this was all secondary.

The reason you went to such a decrepit venue was not to savor the drinks and décor but to stand on the balcony and watch the sun set across the Indian Ocean. There is always something particularly beautiful about watching the sun set over the ocean, but this experience was particularly poignant. On the strip of land between the bar and the ocean, a group of kids were playing soccer. Despite not wearing shoes and playing on rough, broken ground, they managed to play with some skill and sufficient control not to end up kicking their ball into the water.

Beyond the game of kick about, in a scene that has not changed for hundreds of years, dhows sailed gracefully past. These traditional sailing vessels have ploughed the established trading routes between East Africa, the Arabian Peninsula, and the Indian subcontinent for centuries. It was not just the beauty of the sunset, but this feeling of witnessing a link in a long chain of human history, that so caught my imagination that evening.

Not long after the sun had set there was a serious disturbance inside as the bar had run out of beer! A core group of drinkers were close to rioting because they had come to the bar with the intention of settling in for a long drinking session and now claimed they had nowhere else to go.

I took this as my cue to leave.

Although I have enjoyed a drink in my time, I have never understood why people travel so far around the world just to spend most of their time drinking in a hostel bar with other backpackers, rather than getting out and making the most of their time.

I managed to slip out to the evening markets down by the quayside. The markets were a mixture of stalls selling curios; "My friend, would you like to look at this walking stick? Look you turn the handle and you draw out a sword!" as well as some street entertainment and a range of stalls selling local street foods.

It was the food stalls that I had come out for.

There were stalls selling sugar cane juice, with the cane pulped through a hand-operated crusher while you waited. Other stalls sold fresh fish and octopus, barbecued and served on a piece of flat bread. But the stalls that most attracted my senses were the ones selling pilau rice. Batches of the rice were cooked up in huge steel pans, and the rich, aromatic scent of the spices drew me in as the smell of cinnamon and cloves sweetened the warm, humid night air.

Sitting down by the seaside gorging on a large serving of the delicious fragrant rice with pieces of chicken, potatoes, and raisins was one of my most memorable experiences ever of eating street food. The location and vibrancy of the market, the style of the food, and the fact that this experience was finally fulfilling my childhood fantasy of visiting Zanzibar, meant that I went to bed that night feeling at peace.

However, that would all change the next morning.

"You should not go out today. There has been an outbreak of cholera."

I think when the manager of the guesthouse made this announcement we all felt an initial wave of panic. I definitely felt sickened for about an hour or so by the news. How many people had I come into contact with last night at the market? I had eaten food at the market – OK, the food had been hot, but what about the container and fork I had been provided with? Thank goodness I had decided to play it safe and drink a Coke rather than have one of the freshly made juices. Wasn't cholera one of those diseases that struck you hard and killed you quickly? Didn't cholera kill heaps of people in London during the nineteenth century? And we were stuck on an island! What would happen if they decided to quarantine the island and we couldn't leave?

For a large part of the day I stayed within the confines of the guesthouse. By mid-afternoon though, I was hungry and did not feel even remotely sick, and was beginning to feel rather cooped up and a bit bored. No one around me seemed to be sick. I couldn't see scenes of panic or people wailing in the street. Exactly how bad could it be?

So I decided to go on a fact-finding trip and source information from the travelers' grapevine at the local backpackers' hang-out. So it was back to the Sunset Bar at Africa House. After climbing the stairs, it was great to walk into the bar, feel the sea breeze, and look out at a blue ocean with a clear blue sky, with the white sails of the occasional dhow providing a contrast to all of the blue.

At the bar, all of the talk was about the cholera outbreak.

A group had formed around a girl who seemed to be speaking with the apparent authority of an expert. She was a nurse (in hindsight, given her apparent age, she had probably just finished training), and after hearing of the outbreak had gone to the hospital to offer her services, which were politely declined. She did find out that the hospital was treating suspected cases with the antibiotic doxycycline. At that point I had heard all I needed to know: this was the same drug I was taking for my anti-malaria medication. Suddenly, I had the feeling of being bullet proof, and I enjoyed my warm beer while watching the sunset. I noticed though, that the kids were not having their evening game of kick about.

I went down to the evening market but the entire area was deserted. The government had shut it down until further notice. I ended up going back to the guesthouse and having an early night.

The next day I awoke early and decided to properly explore the Stone Town.

Although a settlement has existed at the site for many hundreds of years, the first stone houses were only built during the nineteenth century. This development occurred as a result of the Sultan of Oman, who controlled Zanzibar as well as parts of mainland East Africa, moving from Muscat to Stone Town. The buildings in this area reflect the many influences of the different ethnic communities that have lived here: Omani Arab, Persian, Indian, African, and European.

Walking around, it is hard not to get carried away romanticizing about Stone Town. Within a relatively small zone are the crumbling remains of the Portuguese Fort, and within the heart of the town is a maze of narrow alleys lined with houses, shops, bazaars and mosques.

Under the rule of the Sultanate of Oman during the eighteenth and nineteenth centuries, plantations were developed to grow spices and Zanzibar produced cloves, nutmeg, cinnamon, and pepper. However, Zanzibar was also the main trading port for slaves taken from the East African mainland. It is estimated that 50,000 slaves passed annually through the slave markets of Zanzibar in the mid-nineteenth century.

While watching the dhows sailing on the ocean, seeing the elaborate buildings in Stone Town and reminiscing about the Zanzibar's heyday, it is easy to forget that much of this wealth was built on human misery. Ultimately, a part of Britain's rationale for exerting control over Zanzibar during the nineteenth century was to facilitate the abolition of the slave trade.

Later, while admiring some of the famous finely carved and decorated wooden doors in the Stone Town, I was confronted with my second sobering realization of the day. An army transport crawled past down the narrow road. In the back were piled around ten coffins as well as soldiers wearing surgical masks. The grim awareness then dawned on me was that while I had been arrogantly sitting back drinking beer and thinking that I was "bullet proof," as well as feeling annoyed that the evening markets had been closed down, people had been dying because they did not have access to the medication that I could so easily afford.

Even now, I look back on that day with a mixture of guilt, shame, and horror.

The following recipe best captures the tastes I remembered from the pilau rice that I ate while on Zanzibar. The dish is common throughout the Middle East as well as in western Asian countries such as Turkey, Afghanistan, India and Pakistan. The dish was brought to Africa by the Arabs. In many ways, the cooking technique is similar to that for making risotto or paella.

What I especially like about this dish is its use of spices, and the smell of this dish reminds me of the smells of the spice plantations that I visited while on Zanzibar.

The Hungry Traveller's Spice Island Pilau – serves 4

Shopping List
½ tsp. cumin seeds
½ tsp. whole black peppercorns
3 whole cloves
1 cinnamon stick
4 cardamom pods (or a few pinches ground cardamom)
olive or vegetable oil
2 cloves of garlic
2 tsp. fresh ginger
3 cups of rice
2 chopped onions
900g (2 lbs.) of chicken cut into bite-sized pieces
Chicken stock
2 chopped tomatoes
4 potatoes cut into 1 inch pieces
2/3 cup of raisins

Preparation

Step 1:

Take the spices (cumin, peppercorns, cloves, cinnamon and cardamom) and wrap them in a piece of cheesecloth. Tie off the bundle and place it into a cup of warm water.

Step 2:

Finely chop the garlic and ginger and place to one side.

Step 3:

Heat the oil in a large oven proof pot. Soften the onions and then add the garlic and ginger. Continue stirring on a high heat until the aromas of the ingredients have been released.

Step 4:

Add the chicken and cook until it is browned. Reduce the heat and simmer for a few minutes. Remove the chicken and the onions, and set them aside. Add the rice into the pot and stir it thoroughly to coat each grain of rice with oil. Stir in the spice infused water. Wait a few minutes until the rice has absorbed the liquid, and then add the tomatoes and some of the stock. Cover the pot and simmer for a few minutes, stirring occasionally.

Step 5:

Check the rice every few minutes to see if more stock is needed and stir in extra liquid as necessary. As the rice begins to soften, add the potatoes and raisins and add back the chicken and onions.

Step 6:

Keep the pot covered and simmer for around ten minutes. Continue to check and keep adding stock as required.

Step 7:

Remove the pot from stove and place the covered pot in a

warm oven for 10 to 20 minutes. The dish will be complete once all the liquid has been absorbed by the rice, the chicken is cooked through and the potatoes are cooked.

The Best Homemade Pasta

Location: La Spezia, Italy

Not all of my food inspired travel memories occurred while I was an adult.

When I was six, I traveled with my family to Italy to meet my grandparents for the first time. I remembered that my Nonna and Nonno's apartment was dominated by a large kitchen area, which contained an enormous kitchen table that must have been able to seat ten to twelve people easily. The kitchen, and in particular the kitchen table, was the center of the apartment and the proceedings around lunch dominated daily activities. Every day the extended family, including my uncle, aunt, and cousins, would descend on my grandparents' place for the main meal of the day, arriving during the final stages of food preparation. After the food was served and eaten, there would be coffee and a lot of conversation. It was easily a two-hour ritual.

Without fail, the daily meal consisted of pasta with a simple, traditional tomato sauce. Once a week, or on special occasions, the sauce was cooked with a large piece of beef in it and the slow-cooked meat would be set aside and carved up for dinner that night. However, one thing that was always consistent was that the pasta was always homemade, and making it was the ritual that belonged to my Nonno.

Every morning after the breakfast dishes were cleared away I would sit expectantly at the table. My Nonno would then fold up the tablecloth to expose the table's worn wooden surface. He would then begin the process of making the pasta while my Nonna prepared the sauce.

First he would bring out the flour and scatter some across the table's surface. He would then empty the rest of the bag into an enormous mound. Next, he would place two eggs on the table and pour some water into a cup. Then he would make a well in the top of the mound of flour, crack the two eggs and place both the yolks and whites into the bottom of the well. At this stage, I would be allowed to help, as my Nonno would let me slowly pour in the water until he called out "Basta!" once he had enough. He would break the egg yolks with his thumb and forefinger before working the ingredients by hand into a soft ball of floury dough. Finally, he would start to thump, stretch, and roll the dough, and each time he did so it would become stretchier and stretchier. It was not until later in life that I realized that this was the process of kneading, and that what was making the dough become more elastic was the gluten. As a young kid I thought it was amazing seeing this process.

After the kneading was finished, he would put the smooth-looking ball of dough to one side and set up the pasta machine. Essentially this was a set of rollers that were operated by turning a handle. The device was clamped to the table for stability. I would watch transfixed as my Nonno would break off a small ball of dough and begin the process of folding and rolling and folding and rerolling the dough through the settings of the machine to produce long, thin sheets of pasta. Once he had finished making the pasta sheets, he would fix an additional rolling attachment that would then cut the long sheets into strands of fettuccine. The cut pasta would then be arranged into a series of coils on the floured table until it was time for it to be cooked.

Watching my Nonno make pasta every day is one of two strong memories that I have of him. The other, was of him sitting down with me one rainy afternoon and teaching me to play an Italian card game called *Scorpa*. I could not speak Italian and he could not speak English, but somehow he managed to patiently teach me the relatively complex rules of the game.

Sadly, after that trip I never saw him again. Although my Nonna flew over a number of times to visit, he could not fly and he passed away before I was old enough to travel by myself.

However, quite often when I cook pasta I think back to those times when I used to sit at the kitchen table watching real pasta being made, and silently admonish my laziness as I empty a packet of store bought pasta into the boiling water.

There are a multitude of recipes for creating pasta dough. In general, they vary in terms of the number of eggs versus water that is used. In general, more eggs, or more specifically, using just the yolks, will make a richer pasta that is yellow in color. Some recipes state that oil should also be added as an ingredient. I personally have never seen anyone in my family use oil when making pasta.

The following is a fairly typical egg and flour pasta recipe.

The Hungry Traveller's Homemade Egg Pasta – serves 4 to 6

Shopping List
> 600g (1.3 lbs.) '00' flour
> 6 large eggs (or use 8 egg yolks for a richer pasta)
> Pasta rolling machine with cutting attachment

Preparation

The preparation is quite similar to what I described in my story.

Step 1:
Beat the eggs in a small bowl.

Step 2:
Place the flour on a large board in a mound. Make a well in the center and pour in the beaten egg mixture. Mix the eggs and flour by hand until is the ingredients are combined into a single lump of dough.

Step 3:
Knead the dough. This involves bashing the dough with the heal of the hand into the table, stretching it, reshaping it and constantly repeating the process. The pasta is kneaded once it feels smooth instead of rough and floury.

Step 4:
Wrap the dough in cling film and put it in the fridge to rest.

Step 5:

Clamp the pasta machine to the work surface. Dust the work surface with some flour, take a lump of pasta dough the size of an orange and flatten it. Set the pasta machine at its widest setting - and roll the lump of pasta dough through it. Lightly dust the pasta with flour if it sticks. Fold the pasta in half and roll the dough through again. Repeat this process several times.

Step 6:

Work the dough through all the settings on the machine, from the widest down to the narrowest.

Step 7:

Once the pasta is in a long thin sheet, it can either be cut into sheets for use in lasagne, rolled into tubes for cannelloni or used to make ravioli. Alternatively, run the sheet through a cutting attachment to make pasta such as fettuccine.

Step 8:

Once the pasta has been shaped, lay it on a damp clean tea towel until it is ready to cook.

Tea and the Art of Negotiation

Location: North Africa, Middle East, Turkey

Perhaps it is because most of my travel through North Africa, the Middle East, and Turkey has been by myself. Maybe I look like a fool who is easily parted from his money. Or maybe it is because I look so uncomfortable shopping. But whenever I am in a souk or bazaar I seem to be a favorite target for local traders.

It always starts with the same innocuous, friendly invitation:

"My friend, come into my shop and have a cup of mint tea/apple tea/tea."

From what I have observed, most tourists react with some combination of embarrassment and scepticism when they first hear those words, and I was no different. Indeed, most will never take up the invitation, despite the storekeeper's polite insistence, and some people will just ignore the existence of the storekeeper completely, bow their heads, and burrow on past.

I think that this is a great shame (and walking straight past and ignoring someone who is trying to talk to you is just plain rude).

As a result of mass tourism in some parts of the world, it can be difficult enough at times to feel that you are in another country (apart from perhaps the change in weather). Interacting with local people is one of the last bastions of the travel experience. It is one of the last ways left to try and understand the culture and the country that you are visiting. Trying to speak with random local people in the street will only scare them off (although you would be surprised how often local people, especially children or the elderly will try speak to you when you are sitting down somewhere and you look like a tourist).

Therefore, the next best thing is to interact with the storekeepers and to take them up on their offer of tea. You can be upfront and say that you are not interested in buying any of their wares, and most of the time they will still be happy enough to have you in their shop and to at least try pitch their products to you, or to use your presence in the shop to help entice in other, more weary tourists!

In general, no matter what country you are in, the same sequence of events will be played out once you enter the shop.

First, the owner will introduce himself and offer you a seat and then some tea. In Morocco this was invariably mint tea. In Egypt it was black tea. And in Turkey it was either apple tea or black tea. The owner will then nod to an assistant (that is quite often the barker who convinced you to come into the shop in the first place), who will go to the door and motion to a ten to twelve year old boy. The boy then takes the order and reappears within a few minutes with a tray full of drinks.

While waiting for the tea to arrive, there is a

general exchange of small talk and patter to gain your initial confidence.

"Where are you from, my friend?"

"Ahhh, that is a beautiful country!"

"Oh, have you been?"

"Well, no, but I have heard... Are you sure you are not Berber/from Alexandria/have Turkish parents?"

Nice recovery. These guys are real pros!

The tea then arrives. Before taking my first sip, I like to ask what the custom for toasting is. This always seems to generate a genuinely enthusiastic response and, depending on the country, we are soon clinking glasses to a chorus of *şerefe* (Turkish for *to your honor*), *Fisehatak* (Arabic for *to your health*), or *B'saha* (Moroccan for *to your health*).

Now that the ice has been broken, the storekeeper will be keen to start showing you his wares.

There are some golden rules that I have worked out in my time from my past dealings with store owners in souks and bazaars. I think the five most useful things to remember are the following:

Rule 1:

If the barker drumming up business outside the store asks whether you will come back later, never say "yes" unless you mean it, and never promise to come back thinking that you have successfully gotten the guy off your back. I don't know how, but these guys will always remember your face, and if you walk past them later they can be quite hostile if you still refuse to go into their shop. Saying "maybe" does not really work either, because you will then be asked if that means "maybe yes!" The best follow-up if you are still getting pestered after saying "maybe" is to say Insha'Allah if you are in an Arabic-speaking country. It is, after all, God's will if you return to their store.

Rule 2:

If you say that you like an object (and sometimes, with more aggressive storekeepers, just asking for the price is construed as saying that you like an object), it is assumed that you will purchase it if the price is agreeable. Not buying the object after agreeing on a price will cause an argument.

Rule 3:

Always barter (obviously, don't go overboard for a trinket, unless you really feel it is overpriced). Part of the fun of being in a market is bartering.

Rule 4:

Don't get too upset if you purchase an object from the market and realize later on that you probably paid far too much. This happens to most of us. Just remember that when you made the purchase you were happy with the agreed price, and in a few months you will have completely forgotten how much you paid but will still own the object and be enjoying it. So don't let it spoil your travels now!

Rule 5:

Be patient and enjoy the experience. If it is offered, accept the store owner's hospitality. Negotiations for more expensive items will take time and require patience. Remain polite and don't get frustrated and lose your temper. If you cannot agree on a price, then it was not meant to be. Likewise, if the store owner shows you all his wares and there is nothing that appeals to you, then there is no harm in thanking him for his time and leaving.

It is at the last rule where you can learn most about the people you are dealing with. My experience with these negotiations (at least with more expensive items) is that once you have identified something you like, the sales process completely changes.

I remember once being convinced to enter one of the many rug shops in the Grand Bazaar in Istanbul, Turkey. After sipping on apple tea and seemingly being shown not only every rug in that shop, but also the inventory of the neighboring shops, I saw one that finally caught my interest. Where once there had been what looked like a hundred rugs lying on the floor, within minutes, they were all packed up and put away. The only thing on show, the only object of focus, was the rug that I had selected as my favorite.

"So, how much are you asking for this rug?"

(Price is never discussed until you have said you have shown serious interest.)

"How much would you like to pay?"

"I don't know. I did not intend to buy a rug today."

Yes, I will admit it. I got swept away by the salesmanship – but to be fair to myself I had picked out a carpet with a fairly unique design.

"OK. How about I give you this price?"

He showed me a figure on his calculator screen. A price

never seems to be said out loud, but is always typed onto the screen of a calculator.

"My friend, is your calculator upside down?"

There was laughter at my bad joke. Until the deal is complete, I would no doubt be the funniest person they had ever met. However, rather than discuss the price further, the topic of conversation was changed.

"Look at this picture. Bill Clinton visited my shop when he came to Turkey."

A large framed picture is pulled out from behind a counter. The photo is of the store owner grinning next to the highly coiffed figure of Bill Clinton. It doesn't look like a cardboard cut-out.

"Did you sell him a rug when he came into the store?"

I thought it was a pretty obvious comment to make, but he seemed slightly thrown.

"No, he was only here for a short time to visit the shop."

"So why did he visit your shop? There are so many shops here."

As it transpired, despite the number of shops in the bazaar, most are owned by a handful of families. His family had the right political connections, so when Bill Clinton was scheduled to have a thirty minute visit to the Grand Bazaar, he visited that shop.

"Now this rug is a beautiful piece and I want you to be happy and give you a good price."

(More furious tapping on the calculator.)

"Sorry, when you said give me a good price, I thought you meant a good price for me, not a good price for you!"

Then I was introduced to the assistants in the shop, who

up until that point had been completely ignored. They were all related to the owner. Some discussion ensued about how this was a family business going for generations, before the conversation moved back to the price as he tried to coax an improved counter-offer out of me.

After an hour I had learned just about everything I could ever know about his business, his family, and his family life (likewise he knew most of my life history).

Finally, after an hour and a half, a deal was reached.

A few days later I found out that I had paid way more than I had to for the rug. If only I had been more patient, and a tougher negotiator!

But as I sit here writing this, I look around my room at the things that I have purchased while traveling. Most are things I had no intention of ever buying, and, no doubt, paid too much for: my Turkish rug from the Grand Bazaar in Istanbul, a two-foot tall, intricately inlaid wooden vase from Essaouira in Morocco and a shisha pipe from Aswan in Egypt are just a few of the items.

Yet what I now remember is not how much I paid for these objects.

I look at them and what I remember is my time traveling to the place where each object came from. I also remember the time spent drinking tea for a few hours while trying to negotiate a deal. But what I think about most are the insights that I gained about the life and customs of the people of these places where these items came from.

The following is a recipe for fairly authentic-tasting mint tea.

I once witnessed mint tea being made in Morocco at a place called Ait Benhaddou, famed for its ksar, or fortified city, which lies along the old caravan route between the Sahara and Marrakech. As an aside, the area is quite recognizable, having been used as a location for a number of movies including: *Lawrence of Arabia, The Man Who Would be King, The Jewel of the Nile, The Last Temptation of Christ, The Mummy, Gladiator, Alexander and Kingdom of Heaven.*

This recipe is based in part on my recollection of that demonstration, and my attempts to try recreate it once I got back home!

The Hungry Traveller's Moroccan Mint Tea – serves 6

Shopping List
10 sprigs fresh mint
3 tsp. green tea
3 tbsp. sugar (or adjust according to taste)
4 cups of water

Preparation
Step 1:
Boil the water and pour a small amount in the teapot, swishing it around to warm the pot.
Step 2:
Put the mint, green tea and sugar into the teapot. Fill the teapot with the rest of the hot water.

Step 3:

Let the tea brew for a few minutes.

Step 4:

Set out the glasses for the tea. If you do not have the traditional glasses used for tea, a shot glass could be used instead.

Step 5:

Fill one glass with the tea and pour the tea back into the pot. Repeat the process until the sugar is dissolved.

Step 6:

Pour the tea into the glasses. An authentic glass of mint tea should have foam on its surface once it has been poured. To achieve this, pour the tea with the teapot as high a distance as possible above the glasses – this is quite tricky and show be left to experienced tea pourers only.

Step 7:

Enjoy, and be sure to toast each other with "B'saha" or "to your health!"

Island of Atlantis

Location: Santorini, Greece

Chances are that if you see a picture of the Greek Islands, it will be of whitewashed rendered stone buildings, set against the contrasting backdrop of the blue sea. There is also a good chance that the picture will have been taken in Santorini.

The islands that make up Santorini are unique. They are essentially the remains of an enormous volcanic explosion that occurred around 3,500 years ago, known as the Minoan or Thera eruption. The result was that what had once been a single island, became a ring of islands around a volcanic caldera (a giant central lagoon).

The western edge of the main island forms a dramatic, sheer cliff coastline towering up to 300 yards over the caldera below. The main towns of the island are perched on the crest of the cliff, including Fira, the capital. To the east, the land slopes outwards towards the island's beaches on the Aegean Sea.

Apart from physically transforming the island, the eruption also wiped out a flourishing civilization that existed on the island; the evidence of which is still being steadily uncovered by archaeologists. It is also believed that the destruction caused by this eruption was also the source of the legend of Atlantis.

The massive volcanic eruption is believed to have created a gigantic tsunami that hit the island of Crete to the south which is believed to have indirectly led to the eventual collapse of the Minoan civilization.

The scenery of the cliff top towns is dramatic. The western cliff face of the main island forms an arc that curves around the caldera. From various vantage points along the coast it is possible to see clusters of whitewashed buildings, clinging to or even cut into the side of the cliff face, with a sheer drop down to the blue water of the caldera below.

The water in the caldera is nearly 400 yards deep, making it a safe harbor for shipping. This, combined with the natural beauty of the island's villages, makes it a popular day trip destination for cruise ships during the summer months.

My hotel balcony overlooked the caldera, and every morning I would eat my breakfast and watch up to four cruise ships steam in each day. By mid-morning, swarms of launches would be running back and forth like a trail of ants between the cruise ships and the old port that lies at the bottom of the cliff directly beneath Fira.

Then the thousands of day trippers would make their way from the base of the cliff up to the town, some 300 yards directly above the port.

A few of them would elect to walk in the heat, up the steep path (which included 600 odd steps) that snaked its way from the harbor to the town. The bar located at the top of these steps did a good trade relieving the thirst of these more intrepid tourists, who could sit back with a cold Mythos beer and overlook the harbor in the distance below. Many more would take a donkey ride to the top. However, most would ride by cable car and be up in Fira within minutes!

By midday the old narrow streets of the town would be swollen with people. Canvassers outside every shop would neatly direct the influx of day tourists out of the heat into their restaurants, cafes, and bars overlooking the sparkling blue caldera, or into their air-conditioned shops selling things ranging from trinket souvenirs to local handicrafts and expensive, upmarket jewelry.

For those staying on the island, the quieter, eastern side of the island beckoned, with its beaches and chilled out beachside restaurants.

Although it was possible to access these beaches by public bus, these could get very crowded. The alternative I chose was to rent a quad bike to travel the short distance to the beach and to better explore the rest of the island. Despite the island's small size, there are beaches with different colored sand or pebbles depending on which geological layer is exposed at the shore. The island is home to the Red Beach (which always seemed to be overcrowded), the Black Beach, and the White Beach.

After parking the quad bike by the beach, it is well worth renting a beach chair and umbrella. Most of these concessions are linked to one of the beach-side cafes or restaurants, so without even having to move, there is someone all too happy to take your order. That way, you can spend the day sipping on ice-cold watermelon juice or beer, or lie back in a beach chair and be lulled into an afternoon nap by the lapping of the waves against the shore.

By mid to late afternoon, the horns of the cruise ships begin echoing around the caldera, warning passengers to make their way back. The surge of humanity on the streets of Fira begins to thin out, as the ships slip away one by one into the softening light; the day trippers on-board being blissfully unaware that they are about to miss the most magical part of being on Santorini, watching the sunset over the caldera.

Many people head to Oia, in the north of the island, and cram into the narrow lanes and sit on steps (and any other available patch of land), to watch the sun set directly over the sea. It is an experience worth having. Oia is definitely a town worth visiting, if only to sample the milk pie that is sold at the bakery! For those who suffer from vertigo, I would also recommend not sitting by the window of the bus, as part of the road runs directly above the cliff face.

However, back in Fira the rituals around the sunset and the evening are a bit less casual. People go back to their hotels to get ready for the evening. Although smart casual attire is appropriate, beachwear is definitely frowned on in the cafes and restaurants during the evening.

Sunset time in Santorini seems to be the only hour of the day when everything and everyone, stops moving. There are a multitude of ways to enjoy the sunset. However, to not make the time to sit back and enjoy this part of the day is a waste.

My favorite way to enjoy the sunset was to go to my favorite restaurant in Fira, a first story Greek restaurant called Ampelos. We would arrive a good thirty minutes before sunset and get a table directly overlooking the caldera. As the light begins to fade, the atmosphere of the town visibly relaxes. Increasing numbers of couples wander arm in arm along the main path overlooking the caldera, taking in the ever-changing light and view, as the island starts to put on its most famous show.

And when in Greece, there is only one thing to eat at this time of day, meze. This is a collection of small dishes of food served with piles of pita bread. The beauty of ordering meze is that it allows you to sample the different tastes and produce of the area, as well as the traditional Greek staples. Every evening I would order the same core group of dishes: cheese saganaki (fried Greek cheese with a squeeze of lemon juice), calamari, barbecue octopus, tzatziki (a yogurt dip with cucumber and garlic), Greek salad, and fava dip (a yellow lentil dish unique to Santorini). Complementing all of this would be a bottle of chilled local white wine.

Sitting back, sipping wine and nibbling on the food, time seems to slow down. The sun turns to yellow, and then darkens into a deep orange as it dips further towards the horizon and shimmers in the heat haze. At the same time the sky is cast into a soft orange color, and the azure of the caldera starts to darken and turn purple. Then, as complete silence descends on the town, the sun slips below the horizon. The sky turns an orange-red, before turning purple, and then completely dark.

As if on cue, life returns to the town. The lights go on in the restaurant. There is a bit of a chill in the evening air. Where there were once a few couples standing and looking out across the caldera, people have started streaming onto the main path looking for somewhere to eat. The canvassers are back out again, showing potential customers their menus and trying to convince them that they have the best food in town. The restaurant we are seated in suddenly fills, and is now full of activity as the waiting staff swing their way through the crowded tables.

However, the magic of the evening does not end here.

After eating, a stroll around the town is a must. The shopkeepers are now sitting outside their shops, enjoying the cooler evening air, drinking their espresso, and relaxing after a long, busy day of trying to sell their wares to the day trippers from the cruise ships. I am amazed at how many jewelry shops are located in the town. The last thing I would think of buying while on vacation is an expensive item of jewelry, but then Santorini has traditionally catered to a more upmarket type of traveler (compared with the other places that I typically visit).

Although it is late in the evening, the storekeepers are still keen to engage you as a passer-by and make a potential sale, but it is in a far more relaxed way. They know that they have a few days in which to make a sale because you are staying on the island and are happy to build a rapport. A lot of the store owners are actually Athenians who own jewelry workshops in the Greek capital. They spend their summers on the island selling their wares to tourists, and then during the low season shutter up their businesses and go back to Athens for the winter months. After chatting with one of them, I even feel relaxed enough to promise to come back and look in their shop the next evening!

The caldera is now shrouded in complete darkness. If you are lucky and happen to be there while there is a full moon, you can see the moonlight reflecting off the smooth, inklike water. Looking up along the coast, where during the day one could see clusters of whitewashed buildings stretching along the cliff top, the view has now been replaced with soft twinkling lights running up and down the length of the coast.

At this point you have to stop, stand still, and take in the seeming perfection of it all. This is because it is one of those moments that you will never again experience anywhere else.

The following is a recipe for Fava, a traditional dish of Santorini, made with yellow shelled lentils. It is a dish often served in tavernas and restaurants on the island as a meze-style dip.

The Hungry Traveller's Fava Dip – serves 4

Shopping List
1 cup of fava lentils
2 - 2 ½ cups water
1 small onion
Olive oil
½ a lemon
Salt
Pita bread

Preparation
Step 1:
Wash the fava lentils. Place the lentils in a saucepan with the water and cook on a medium heat. The amount of water

added should create a mixture resembling a thick paste.

Step 2:

Keep checking on and stirring the fava. If required, add further water to ensure that the mixture does not dry out.

Step 3:

After around 10 minutes of cooking, add the roughly chopped onion.

Step 4:

When the fava lentils have softened they are cooked. Remove them from the heat and add salt to taste.

Step 5:

Blend or mash the mixture into a paste.

Step 6:

Serve with a drizzle of olive oil, a squeeze of fresh lemon and pita bread.

An Australian Classic?

Location: Sydney, Australia

When you think of Sydney, Australia, there are certain iconic images that come to mind. Most of them we have seen on television commercials or in books: the white sails of the Opera House floating across the deep blue harbor, with the steel arch of the Sydney Harbour Bridge in the background. And, of course, all of it is bathed in sunshine. Alternatively, there is the image of the white sands of Bondi Beach patrolled by deeply tanned lifeguards with chiseled jaws, living an idealized existence of surf, sand, and sun.

Likewise, when asked about Australian foods, people usually think of "bush tucker" such as witchetty grubs, goanna, and kangaroo.

When visiting Sydney I was struck by the fact that it does look as spectacular as in the ads and documentaries I had seen on TV. As I watched office workers descend on the area around Circular Quay at lunchtime, it was hard not to feel envious of the "Sydney Lifestyle." People would sit on benches with their sandwiches looking out across the harbor, or in the green spaces enjoying the sun. A significant number even had the energy to go for a lunchtime jog along the harbor foreshore. However when you see a map of

Sydney and realize that it is home to over 4.5 million people and more than 600 sprawling suburbs out to the north, west, and south of central Sydney, it becomes clear that this harborside lifestyle is only routinely enjoyed by a fraction of the population.

For the most part Sydney is very much a modern city with a high-rise skyline dominating the central business district. Even standing down at Circular Quay, which is the tourist gateway to exploring the city's iconic sights such as the "Harbour", the "Bridge", the "Opera House", and the historic district of The Rocks, you feel as if you are in the shadow of the imposing skyline. This is because despite there being an indigenous occupation in Sydney dating back 30,000 years, little visible evidence of this now remains. And given that the British colony was not established until 1788, the oldest surviving buildings only date back to the nineteenth century.

The Rocks district was established not long after the foundation of the colony and was originally a sandstone block quarry. From the beginning, the area had the reputation for being a slum. During the nineteenth century it was often an area operating outside the law, controled by gangs and the haunt of prostitutes catering to traveling sailors. In the early part of the twentieth century, large parts had been subject to redevelopment and demolition (including large areas being demolished to facilitate the construction of the Sydney Harbour Bridge).

The area was constantly at risk of being demolished until the 1970s, when what remained was protected once and for all, after government plans for demolition and redevelopment were opposed by local residents and trade unions placing a 'Green Ban' on carrying out the proposals.

The area today consists of nineteenth century buildings and warehouses that have been converted into galleries, souvenir shops, and restaurants. However, one type of original establishment still retains its historical links to the past - the district's bars. In fact, there is a hotly contested rivalry between a number of the bars, as to which was the first in Sydney.

To me this was one of the great things about The Rocks. It might not be the most glorious claim to fame, and it is doubtful that the dispute would ever be discussed in history textbooks but the owners and patrons of each of the contender bars are very passionate about their claim to being the oldest establishment in Sydney. OK, it may not be the Pantheon in Rome with its 2,000 years of continuous history, but these businesses have been in continual operation since the earliest days of the colony. From that perspective at least, I felt that they represent a real connection with Sydney's past that was lacking in the more gentrified areas of The Rocks.

And as much as it seems to be a cliché about Australia, the fact that it is a group of bars that have survived the area's colorful beginnings, its period of gang rule, outbreaks of the plague, and constant threats of the developer's wrecking ball, seems somehow fitting.

So what is the oldest bar in Sydney? The honest answer is that no one knows for sure because all of these places were in operation well before liquor licensing! But it was a fun day drinking at the different establishments trying to find out. And if you want to seem like a local, go into a bar serving Tooheys beer on tap and ask for a 50-50, which is half a schooner of Tooheys Old topped with a half of Tooheys New.

As easy as it would be to have concluded with my experiences of Sydney in the front bar of one of the bars in The Rocks district, this wasn't my unique Sydney experience.

That distinction belongs to the time I ate Sydney rock oysters down on the beachfront at Watson's Bay.

I was told to visit Watson's Bay because it was an area less visited by tourists but which could still be reached by catching a ferry across Sydney Harbour. I relished the idea of catching one of the small green and yellow (or on reflection was it meant to be green and gold?) commuter ferries, where I could lean over the railings and see Sydney properly from the water, free from having to jostle with other tourists for a space overlooking the railings, as I had on an earlier ferry trip to Manly.

Watsons Bay is a fairly quaint harborside suburb in eastern Sydney. It is in a unique location, sitting on the end of the South Head peninsula at the entrance to Sydney Harbour. The ferry docks on the harborside of the peninsula at a sheltered bay from which the area takes its name. From here it is possible to walk from the harborside village along a path to South Head and out to an area called The Gap, an ocean side cliff overlooking the Pacific Ocean and, tragically, a notorious suicide location.

Along from the ferry jetty and right on the beach at Watson's Bay is a Sydney institution, Doyle's on the Beach. Doyle's has operated a seafood restaurant from this location since the late nineteenth century. This place is well worth a visit just to experience the location. Sitting outside in the sunshine, the water gently lapping the yellow-white sand of the beach just a few yards away, and with magnificent views back towards Sydney, it seems a world apart from the hustle and bustle of the city, which is only a few miles away.

Up until my visit to Watson's Bay, on the few occasions that I had eaten oysters, I had always eaten them raw with some lemon juice. I had always thought that adding anything else just seemed a bit too fussy. However, as I was ordering some oysters I was told by the waitress that I should try them in the local "Kilpatrick" style. Despite my misgivings about cooking a fresh oyster, I figured that you should always trust local advice and agreed to try it.

And what was I served? I was presented with a plate of half-shelled oysters with cooked bacon and a brown colored sauce. Yet despite appearances, the oysters were delicious. They were warmed rather than cooked, and the softness of the metallic oyster flesh contrasted with the smoky crispness of the bacon. The flavor of the sauce was also amazing. Even to this day, the memory of eating that dish makes my mouth water.

And the best thing about the entire experience was that I ate some quality, indigenous Australian food in an amazing, relaxed location, and none of it felt like a clichéd TV commercial!

However, although Australians claim Oysters Kilpatrick as their own invention, no one was able to verify where and by whom the dish was first invented! Or perhaps it is like the mystery of the oldest bar in Sydney: does it really matter if it is the oldest or the second oldest bar, so long as it serves a cold beer to relieve your parched throat in good surroundings?

The following is a version of Oysters Kilpatrick that I have actually cooked myself. There are literally dozens of variations to the recipe but all involve oysters (obviously), bacon, and Worcestershire sauce. Although a lot of recipes don't require the bacon to be cooked separately, I feel that this is a necessary step that gives the bacon a crisper texture than would be achieved by just broiling it with the oysters for a minute or two.

The Hungry Traveller's Oysters Kilpatrick – serves 2

Shopping List
> 1 dozen fresh Sydney rock oysters (if you do not live in Australia any fresh oysters in their shell will be fine)
> 1 shallot
> 3 bacon rashers trimmed of fat and rind
> 2 tbsp. tomato sauce (ketchup)
> 6 tbsp. Worcestershire sauce
> 1 tbsp. lemon juice
> ¼ cup shredded Parmesan cheese

Preparation
> **Step 1:**
> Place the opened oysters in their ½ shells on an oven tray.
> **Step 2:**
> Dice up the bacon into tiny cubes and lightly fry.

Step 3:

Chop the shallot into very thin slivers.

Step 4:

Place the cooked chopped bacon, shallots, tomato sauce, and Worcestershire sauce and lemon juice into a bowl and stir thoroughly.

Step 5:

Spoon the mixture over each oyster.

Step 6:

Lightly sprinkle a pinch of Parmesan cheese over each oyster.

Step 7:

Take the tray and broil for a couple of minutes. The oysters should only be heated and not cooked.

Note that other variations to the dish include the addition of Tabasco sauce for a bit of added kick, sautéing onion while frying the bacon (I personally think this adds too many flavors and does not really complement the oyster), as well as adding breadcrumbs into the mix.

Eire of the Dog

Location: Republic of Ireland

OK, despite spending two weeks traveling around Ireland, I cannot recall one memorable meal that I had. Don't get me wrong, I had an amazing two weeks – it is just that for once, none of my memories were associated with food.

But a lot of the good times I had were associated with the nightlife, great pubs (bars) and many pints of Guinness!

Just to be clear, I do not want to make it sound like I spent my entire time in Ireland slumped over a bar. It is a beautiful country and with its lush green countryside, you can see why it is called the "Emerald Isle."

Despite traveling extensively through the western part of the country, which is exposed to the changeable weather off the North Atlantic Ocean, I was fortunate to have relatively good weather during my visit and to see the magnificent Cliffs of Moher bathed in sunshine. The view from the top of O'Brien's Tower was dramatic, looking out as it did over the green undulating fields dropping to a sheer 200 yard plunge to the ocean below. Of course, this was nothing compared to the complete terror I felt when I decided to take a "closer look," and laid myself out flat along the cliff edge, with my head hanging over the cliff, looking straight down at the swirling, bubbling, and crashing surf hundreds of feet below.

No less dramatic are the abandoned farms along the west coast in County Clare. Once, small tenant farmers eked out a frugal existence on tiny plots of land, until the potato blight that resulted in the Great Famine during the mid-nineteenth century. This is believed to have resulted in the deaths of an estimated million people and the emigration at least a further million from Ireland. As a result, it is estimated that the Irish population plummeted by up to twenty-five per cent, with an even more dramatic population loss in areas like County Clare. Today, the grassy, overgrown fields are still marked out with their old stone boundary walls, and the collapsed, single-room stone cottages are the enduring memorials to those who suffered and perished.

Yet I will also remember Ireland for the great times that were had at the end of each day's travel.

I remember arriving in Dublin relatively late on a Friday night and walking into a random pub to find it packed. The first thing I did was order a pint of Guinness at the bar – after all, I was in Ireland! For the uninitiated, Guinness is probably Ireland's most famous export after its people. First brewed by Arthur Guinness in the mid-eighteenth century, it is a dry stout. It is famous for its black color and thick creamy head (although while I was there I found out that officially, the drink is a dark ruby color).

However, one thing to be aware of when ordering a Guinness is that you will need to wait a couple of minutes for it to be poured properly. After the initial pour the beer needs to settle to allow the head to properly develop as the nitrogen gas bubbles out of the beer. Once the beer has settled, it is then topped up before being served.

Given how long I had been traveling to get to Ireland, I felt impatient as I watched my beer settling on the bar. The tempestuous mixture of tiny bubbles swirled within the liquid, making the beer look brown in color. Then, slowly, like a curtain being drawn up on a stage, a layer of black (sorry, dark ruby) liquid formed at the bottom of the glass, increasing in size as the swirling mass of bubbles moved up the glass to eventually form the head on the beer. One of the great paradoxes of watching this show was that the individual bubbles appeared to be moving down the glass, while the overall settling mass of bubbles was in fact moving up the glass!

After the second pour the beer was handed to me and I thirstily gulped down my first mouthfuls and felt that unmistakable sweet/burned/bitter taste as the beer passed over my tongue.

Having been relieved of my initial thirst, I took a look around the pub. It was almost as if I was in the middle of a scene from an Irish tourism commercial. There was a live band on stage playing the distinctive sounds of Irish music. There was a woman singing, a couple of guys playing fiddles, and another playing what looked like some sort of recorder (which I was later to learn was called a whistle). Around the stage were arranged a series of tables. Every seat was taken; the rest of the patrons were standing around the edge of the room watching the band or, like me, were positioned near the bar. What I found most interesting was that by and large most people sat or stood in silence while the musicians performed, and only broke out into conversation once the band was on a break.

During one of the intervals I was engaged by an "old-timer" who asked,

"So, where are you from?"

Clearly he was one of the "regulars" at the pub. I told him where I was from.

"We get a lot of tourists in Ireland."

"Well, it has a reputation for being a beautiful country"

"True, but it has changed a lot in the last thirty years." (the latter pronounced as "tirtee years")

I internally braced myself for a series of stories about the good old days. To change the topic of conversation I offered to buy him a drink and ordered two pints from the bar.

"So, is there normally a band here on a Friday night?"

"There's one here every night. It has always been like this. Despite everything that has changed some things have remained the same…"

Where were those drinks that I had ordered? At least the arrival of the drinks would provide me another excuse for changing the topic of conversation. I was going to have to listen to this guy tell me about everything that was wrong with the world. One universal thing about pubs (or coffee shops, where pubs or the pub culture does not exist), is that there always seems to be one or two opinionated regulars who, having bored the other regular patrons, will latch onto an unsuspecting outsider and deliver their lecture about all the ills of the world. However, this guy was about to make me feel foolish.

"When I grew up we were all dirt-poor and had no opportunities unless we left the country. Ireland has completely changed with the EU. We have big companies in Dublin now and the kids today no longer have to leave for work. Things are so much better."

And as a concession to his place as part of the league of bar "regulars" he added,

"But the cost of a pint has gone through the roof!"

As I recall this conversation many years later, I wonder what he now thinks about Ireland's rapid growth as the *Celtic Tiger*, as the country readjusts to a more austere existence following the collapse of its property market and banking system.

However one thing he mentioned, which I noticed every night, was the culture of live music. No matter how small the town, or what night of the week it was, there was always a live band and an attentive audience at the local pub. And these venues all seemed to be relaxed and informal, with requests being called out from the audience, and even some audience members coming up on stage to sing.

The composition of the band would vary a little but there would almost always be someone playing the fiddle, another playing a whistle or flute, and someone singing. Often there would be other instruments such as the "Irish drum" or bodhrán, as well as guitars and even, once, the Uilleann Pipes or "Irish Bagpipes."

All of these evenings would involve conversations with a lot of random people, and a lot of pints of Guinness. And every morning I would drag myself out of bed, feeling slightly worse for wear, for another day of travel. However, my "hair of the dog" pint at lunchtime did help a lot!

There was one evening that was more memorable than

the others. We had traveled to the Dingle Peninsula, a fairly remote region on the Irish west coast. It is an area that is particularly exposed to the Atlantic, and that night it was cold, windy, and pouring with rain. It was classic weather for going to the local pub, and evidently everyone else staying in the small village had the same idea, for the pub was packed with locals and backpackers alike.

This session was particularly informal, and it appeared that the band had an open mike when it came to who would sing. Almost all the songs were sung were in Gaelic, and when the music became more up-tempo, a group of guys from one of the backpacking trips decided to do their attempt at Irish dancing - with all the results one would expect! The musicians then requested that this group sing a song so that they could take a break. And with a little bit of coaxing from the audience, the group broke out into the chorus of *Waltzing Matilda*, sounding half like a song, and half like some sort of Australian war cry.

This encouraged other "outsiders" up to the microphone, most of it to the hilarity of the locals. However, for me the evening was stolen by one of the girls from the tour group when she sang Pokarekare Ana, the famous Maori love ballad. This girl could obviously sing, and the hauntingly beautiful lyrics made everyone in the room fall into silence.

As I lay back in my bed that night in my inebriated philosophical state, I thought of the two songs from the night that were still stuck in my head, the drunken rendition of Waltzing Matilda and the Maori love song, and how, in at least my state of mind, they could both be linked to the country I was in. Waltzing Matilda is a song of defiance against authority, as the swagman (who quite possibly, like a lot of working-class Australians during the nineteenth century, could have been of Irish descent) would rather die than surrender to the Authorities (who at that time in Australia would most likely have been of English descent). And Pokarekare Ana, although clearly not an Irish song, is nonetheless a hauntingly beautiful and tragic love ballad, that could fit into a lot of the themes of Irish music.

For me, this night stood out because it summed up the cultural experience that I had while in Ireland. There was the friendliness of the local people, and the fact that the music being performed did not seem to belong only to an elite group on stage, but to everyone at the venue, singing along to the ballads that they knew without drowning out the voice of the main performer. They also knew how to have a good "craic," appreciating the humor of the Aussie guys trying to do Irish dance, and bringing them and the rest of us outsiders into their world and culture. And finally, there was that lubricant that bound together my entire Irish experience, a few pints of Guinness.

I realize that it is a cop-out to not have a single memorable food moment after being two weeks in a country, and no doubt my publisher will receive lots of colorful feedback about what a culinary and cultural ignoramus I am. Perhaps so, but these are the experiences that I had. Given my memorable experiences involving Ireland's famous beer, I have decided to include my Steak and Guinness pie recipe.

The Hungry Traveller's Steak and Guinness Pie – serves 4

Shopping List

1 pint of Guinness
½ tbsp. vegetable oil
900g (2 lbs.) chuck or skirt steak cut into chunks
2 finely chopped garlic cloves
1 large diced white onion
2 diced carrots
1 cup of sliced mushrooms
4 beef stock cubes
puff pastry sheets
1 egg
Salt and pepper to taste

Preparation

Step 1:

Heat the oil in a large pot on a high heat. Add in the onion and garlic and briefly stir.

Step 2:

Add the beef and cook until the meat has browned.

Step 3:

Turn down the heat and pour in half the Guinness. Add in the carrots, crumble in the stock cubes and add salt and pepper. If required, add water until all of the meat is covered.

Step 4:

Simmer for approximately one and a half hours until the meat is cooked and tender.

Step 5:

Take the ingredients off the heat and allow them to cool.

Step 6:

Place the meat and gravy mixture into a deep pie dish. Cover with the puff pastry.

Step 7:

Lightly beat the egg yolk, and brush over the pastry.

Step 8:

Put the pie into a medium hot oven for around further twenty minutes.

Step 9:

Once the pastry has puffed and has turned golden brown, it is cooked.

The First Time I Ate Genuine Indian Food?

Location: Little India, Singapore

Before I lived in Singapore, my experience of Indian food was that it was either hot or impossibly hot, full of chilies that provided a lot of heat but little taste. For this reason, eating Indian food was considered a contest of bravery among my family and friends. Eating an entire vindaloo curry earned you the respect of your fellow diners, whereas being a "coward" and eating butter chicken meant humiliation and scorn.

I knew that *real* Indian food had to be better than this. Given the significant Indian population in Singapore, I reasoned that there had to be a number of reasonably priced, good quality Indian restaurants.

At work I asked some local Singaporeans where I should go for good Indian food.

"Little India," was the response.

I had been hoping for an answer that would be a bit more specific, so I patiently asked,

"Where abouts in Little India?"

"All the places along Racecourse Road are pretty good"

"Is there a specific place that you would recommend?"

(I was getting closer.)

"It depends on what you feel like eating."

(False alarm! I was getting further away again.)

"OK, if you were going to go out and eat along Racecourse Road tonight, which restaurant would you eat at?"

After five minutes of caveated explanations (I would learn afterwards in cultural awareness training that as the "boss" I was not supposed to put people who worked with me on the spot like that. This even included asking for a restaurant recommendation, but I digress), I finally got an answer.

"Muthu's"

"OK, thanks."

"I guess if you go to Muthu's, you should eat the fish head curry."

That Sunday, I headed into Little India.

This district of Singapore has roots dating back to the colonial era, when the British adopted a policy of ethnic segregation. Although Little India was not the official area for segregating the predominantly Tamil immigrants, it developed as a "spill over" area due to crowding in the official district of Chulia Kampong.

Although the days of segregation are long gone, the southern Indian influences in Little India are still very strong, with traditional restaurants; specialty shops selling spices, curry, and clothing; mosques; and temples.

Walking along Racecourse Road to get to the restaurant, I passed a wide grass verge adjacent to Farrer Park Field. As it was Sunday, it was the only full day off that most migrant laborers had during the week, and this grassy area was packed with Tamil migrant workers – all of them men, who had spent their day picnicking there. I couldn't help but feel how tough it must be for the migrant semi-skilled and unskilled workers in Singapore. Although they are probably well paid compared with what they would make in their native towns and cities, their real earnings are quite low considering the cost of living in Singapore. To save money, therefore, they live in communal groups apart from their families for extended periods so they can maximize the amount that they can send back home.

After a few more minutes of walking I arrived at Muthu's Curry House. Entering the restaurant, I was somewhat surprised to see it decked out with very modern-looking decor. However, what more immediately grabbed my attention was the fact that although the restaurant had table service, because of the high turnover volume the main dishes were already precooked and on display. This meant that the completely uninitiated (like me) could walk along and see what all of the dishes looked like, rather than play guessing games with the menu. To be honest, all the dishes looked great. However there was only one dish that I was interested in seeing, and that was the fish head curry.

I don't know what I was expecting to see; maybe it was a multitude of small fish heads – I cannot exactly remember anymore. But the "fish head" was essentially a third to a half of a large fish with the head attached, cooked in a thick sauce (although I was later corrected and told that I should use the term *gravy* instead of sauce). I ordered a serving of the fish head curry, some bread, and a Tiger Beer.

The dish soon arrived. The first thing I noticed as it was placed on the table was how fragrant it was. The serving consisted of a deep-sided bowl with a single "fish head" in it (which, as I have already mentioned, was not exactly just a fish head), covered in a generous helping of thick gravy. The fish was quite tasty but the star of the dish was the gravy, which was so delicious that I ordered extra bread to make sure that I scooped it all up.

I will confess that I don't know what the exact flavors were that made the fish taste so good. What most surprised me, though, was that although it was a curry dish, the heat was relatively mild; it did not overpower the more delicate and fragrant components of the sauce that really made the dish quite special.

This may have been my first experience eating fish head curry, but it was definitely not my last. All in all, it was a great introduction into my first taste of authentic southern Indian cooking.

Well that is at least what I thought for over a year.

As I was preparing to leave Singapore, I caught up with a Singaporean friend who had an Indian background for a good bye drink.

As I sat down at the table and handed my friend his drink he asked,

"So what will you miss about Singapore?"

"Well," I replied, "I definitely won't miss the price of alcohol!"

Even after all the time I had been there, I could not get over just how disproportionately expensive alcohol was. However, I had been thinking about that very question for some time. Initially I had a lot of reservations about moving to Singapore. When I had first visited a number of years earlier to see some friends while I was still backpacking, I had found it a bit sterile and uninteresting compared with the other countries in the region that I had just been traveling through.

Yet Singapore had grown on me after a couple of months.

True, it did not have the color and excitement of other countries in the region. However, traveling through a country with infrequent, non-air-conditioned public transport, where eating local street foods can be a bit of a lottery and where you have to brush your teeth using bottled water due to the poor quality of the water supply, is one thing. Once you are back home from traveling, the "little" details, such as the grime and pollution of the big cities, or the smell of dirt and sweat on local public transport, or the fact that for at least a third of the time you were traveling your tummy was never quite right, are all quickly forgotten. Instead, you can wax lyrical about what an accomplished traveler you are (rather than being some "tourist"), and tell all your family and friends about the adventures you had along the way.

As I said, that is all well and good when you are traveling. However, when you are living somewhere, you want to live in a clean city with clean, reliable public transport and a safe water supply. When you work all day, your spare time is far more precious, and you don't want getting from point A to point B to be a time-consuming "adventure." Singapore is a modern, well-functioning city, which might not make it an exotic location to travel to but did make it a good place to live. What I also liked was the city's diversity. Although it may not have always been as harmonious and tolerant as officials like to claim, but each of the various ethnic groups were all passionate about their food, which meant that there was an amazing array of fairly inexpensive restaurants selling really good quality meals.

"So is that your final answer? You won't miss expensive alcohol?"

My self-reflecting had left my friend hanging.

"Sorry, I was just thinking about how much I will miss the food."

"What a surprising answer coming from you!"

Everyone has to be a comedian

"I am serious. I tried many different foods when I was growing up, but a lot of the flavors had been adjusted to reflect local expectations, or to just cover up plain bad cooking. Before coming here I thought Indian food was just about lots of chilies and not much else. Then I went to Muthu's and tried the fish head curry, and for the first time ever realized just how good authentic Indian cooking can be!"

My friend burst out laughing.

"How long have you been spouting off that line about fish head curry being authentic Indian food? It is a Singaporean invention! In fact it was invented at Muthu's, which is why it is the house special there. The story is that the guy who set up the restaurant – whose name by the way is not even Muthu - thought that offering fish heads on the menu would increase the potential appeal of his restaurant to Chinese customers."

I was crestfallen. All this time I thought I had been eating "adventurous" southern Indian cuisine. My friend sensed how this new realization had deflated me and destroyed all of my conceptions about Singapore and its food.

"Well, to be fair the fish head curry is prepared in the style of southern Indian cooking, and you now correctly realize that there is more to Indian cooking adding lots of chilies. Don't try so hard to create some philosophical view about Singaporeans and food. We like to eat good food. I also think it is great that I can eat food similar to the traditional dishes that I grew up with as well as dishes that are completely new to me. After all, where else in the world can you eat chili stingray from a street stall in the early hours of the morning after a big night out?"

I rolled my eyes, thankful that as far as I was aware this was unique to Singapore. No matter how many chilies were used there was nothing that could disguise the tough, stringy stingray flesh. That was one dish I would be happy to see the back of.

Thanks to my friend's final comment, at least I now knew that I could claim to have a balanced view of my food experiences in Singapore. I did not love *every* dish that I had eaten there.

The following is a recipe for making fish head curry. Although this recipe provides a good-tasting dish, it is still not as good as the original one that I ate at Muthu's. The masala that is used as the basis of the gravy at Muthu's is a closely held family secret, that is rumored to be known to only two family members, who make up a batch of it each day. Also, if the thought of having a fish eye staring at you off the plate makes you feel a bit squeamish, using fish fillets will also work fine for this dish.

The Hungry Traveller's Fish Head Curry – serves 6

Shopping List

½ whole fish head (this is basically half a snapper)

1 tbsp. of minced ginger

3 cloves of minced garlic

3 thinly sliced onions

5 tbsp. fish curry powder made into a paste with ½ cup of water (see below for how to make the fish curry powder)

300g (2/3 lb.) okra

3 chopped tomatoes

6 red chilies (cut lengthwise)

2 to 3 sprigs of curry leaves

salt to taste

1 tbsp. sugar

1 tbsp. tamarind mixed with ½ cup of water

1 cup coconut milk

5 tbsp. vegetable oil

Ingredients (fish curry powder):

4 tbsp. coriander powder

1 tbsp. cumin powder

2 ½ tbsp. chili powder

1 ½ tsp. turmeric powder

1 tsp. ground black pepper

½ tsp. fenugreek powder

Preparation

Step 1:

Season the fish and steam it until it is just cooked.

Step 2:

Heat the oil in a saucepan, add the ginger and garlic and cook until softened. Then add the fish curry paste and cook until the fragrant spices have been released.

Step 3:

Add the onions and briefly fry. Put in half of the coconut milk and bring to the boil before adding the remaining coconut milk and tamarind.

Step 4:

Add the okra, tomatoes, red chilies, curry leaves, salt and sugar and simmer to cook the sauce.

Step 5:

When ready to serve, add the fish head and simmer gently until the fish is hot and well cooked. Add extra liquid if more gravy is required.

A Surreal Day

Location: Phnom Penh, Cambodia

I have made countless attempts to write this story, the events of which all transpired in a single day in Phnom Penh in Cambodia. Even all these years later, in terms of what I experienced, and the contrasting emotions that I felt, I still struggle to reconcile the events that occurred within that twelve-hour period, in what was the most surreal day of my life.

Like most tourists, I was traveling to Cambodia with the primary purpose of visiting the awe-inspiring Angkor Wat complex. However, as I had entered Cambodia from the east via Vietnam, I had decided to travel via Phnom Penh and spend a day there before flying out to Siem Reap, the nearest town to Angkor (the roads in Cambodia were diabolically bad back then).

I had made an early start to make the most of my one full day in the Cambodian capital.

I arrived at the Tuol Sleng Genocide Museum as it opened. This site was the notorious Security Prison 21 (S-21) used by the Khmer Rouge from its rise to power in 1975 until its fall in 1979.

When Pol Pot's regime took power, it embarked on a program of mass social engineering, with the objective of creating a purely agrarian society. The cities were emptied of people, who were forced to work on rural agrarian projects. At the same time, "dissidents" and their families were rounded up, including, officials from the previous government and ethnic minorities, as well as anyone deemed to be an "intellectual," such as middle-class academics, doctors, teachers, students, monks, and engineers. Eventually, even members of the regime became victims as a result of purges within the party.

Buildings such as those at Toul Sleng were converted into prisons. At Toul Sleng, what was formerly a high school, had its buildings enclosed with barbed wire, with its classrooms converted into prison cells and torture chambers. Once a person was sent to one of these prisons, the almost inevitable outcome was torture and death. It is estimated that some 17,000 people were imprisoned within S-21. There were only seven known survivors.

What is so chilling about visiting Toul Sleng, is that the buildings are preserved as they were left by the Khmer Rouge, who fled just ahead of the advancing Vietnamese army, leaving behind the extensive records of the victims. Several rooms in the museum are given over to thousands of black and white photographs that line the walls from floor to ceiling. It is incredibly sobering to see the faces of thousands of victims of torture and murder staring silently at you. Many in the photos look distressed, no doubt aware of what their fate was going to be.

The photographs were taken when the prisoners were first brought in. Prisoners would then give their biographies before being stripped to their underwear and taken to crowded cells, where they would be shackled and made to sleep directly on the floor. It is estimated that up to 1,500 people were held in the prison at any one time. Prisoners were typically detained over a two to three month period, and were subjected to systematic abuse consisting of starvation, sleep deprivation, and being prevented from communicating with the other prisoners. They would be beaten for breaching any of the prison rules, and were repeatedly interrogated, coerced, and tortured until confessions were extracted. Most confessions were false, but would often implicate family members, friends and associates, who would in turn be arrested and brought into S-21 to be tortured and killed.

The instruments of torture are on display in the museum. Apart from being beaten, prisoners were subjected to electric shocks, heated metal probes, being cut with knives, and waterboarding.

Apart from the haunting photos of the victims, the most distressing part of the museum for me was one of the rooms that held the last of the prisoners. The room has remained almost untouched since the prison was captured by the Vietnamese. It contains a rusting iron bedframe, with a black and white photo of the room as it was found, complete with the chained and mutilated body of the prisoner who had been killed only hours earlier, by his fleeing captors. Not even the stains in the room have been removed.

Despite the horrific conditions, the deprivation, the beatings, and the torture, prisoners were not allowed to die until their full confessions had been extracted. Only then were they executed.

During S-21's first year of operation, executed prisoners were buried nearby. However, by the end of 1976 the prison had run out of space, and prisoners and their families were transported to the Choeung Ek extermination center.

After finishing at Toul Sleng, I boarded the back of an old truck and bounced along a rutted dirt road for the nine mile trip to Choeung Ek. This location is probably the most infamous of the "Killing Fields" sites that existed all around Cambodia, and a term that gave the name to the highly acclaimed 1984 movie about the Khmer Rouge in Cambodia.

However, nothing could have prepared me for what I was about to see.

As we pulled outside the site, it felt like we were just in an innocuous part of the Cambodian countryside. After entering, however, the first thing that I noticed was a large, white Buddhist stupa. It contains the skulls of over five thousand victims and serves as an official memorial to those who were executed at the Killing Fields. It is believed that the remains of 1.3 million people across some 20,000 mass gravesites are scattered throughout the country.

Walking around the rest of the site, which is effectively a series of mass graves, I was surprised at what a small place it was to be the resting place for so many thousands of people. Before entering, we had been told that if we saw any human remains we should inform an official. The reality, though, was that the site was littered with teeth, bone fragments, and perhaps even more disturbingly, clothing. Even thirty-five years after the last of the executions, remains are frequently washed out of the unexcavated graves every time there is a heavy rain. It was a sight that was both grisly and distressing.

The site also has a number of plaques with short, matter of fact inscriptions, explaining horrific facts to visitors:

The location where trucks would arrive and unload 20 to 30 blindfolded prisoners at a time.

Excavated pits where victims have been exhumed with an occasional sign noting how many victims had been found.

A Chankiri Tree or Killing Tree.

This was perhaps the most disturbing sign of all. Children were executed along with their allegedly dissident parents, so that they wouldn't grow up seeking revenge for their parents' deaths. Children and infants were executed by being repeatedly smashed against such Killing Trees. In fact, due to the large number of people being executed and the shortage of ammunition, just about all the victims who were brought to the Killing Fields were butchered with makeshift weapons such as iron bars, pickaxes or machetes.

Before leaving the site, I took a closer look at the memorial to the victims. Behind the glass were rows and rows of skulls. I noticed that many of the skulls had been shattered or smashed in. After months of fear and torture, even death for those poor people was brutal and bloody.

Returning to the city in the back of the truck, I felt sickened by what I had seen that morning. And looking around it was clear that I was not the only one who had been affected.

Textbooks can give you the terrible statistics. Nobody knows for certain how many people died during the short period when the Khmer Rouge was in power. However, up to 2.5 million people are estimated to have died as a direct result of the regime's policies. Given an initial population of 8 million, in less than four years some twenty-five per cent of the population was killed.

But statistics such as these run the risk of becoming no more than numbers because the loss of human life on such a scale cannot be comprehended when presented as figures on a page. After all, how do you conceptualize the deaths of so many people? My visit to Toul Sleng and the Killing Fields helped to give some context to this enormous tragedy. Whether it be, the rows and rows of photos lining the walls of several rooms, the stained walls and floors of the prison cells, the experience of stepping over the body fragments and clothes of the victims that still wash up after so many years, or reading a sign on tree that says *Chankiri Tree*.

Although many thousands of people died as a result of S-21 and the nearby Killing Fields, it still represents only a tiny fraction of the total number of people who were exterminated across thousands of sites in Cambodia. Sadly, although this was one of the bloodiest acts of genocide in human history, these atrocities seem to have now been forgotten by the outside world.

When I returned to my hotel at around lunchtime, I noticed some hawkers outside the front gate. They were trying to convince passing tourists to go on one of their motorcycle tours around the city.

"Motor bike tour only 4,000 riel"

I could see the headlines now. "Backpacker, last seen getting on the back of stranger's motorcycle." But he was only charging the equivalent of a dollar. He was also a lot smaller than me...

"But 4,000 is the cost of a full-day tour. It is after lunch; I will give you 2,000"

He laughed and turned to face the other motorcycle tour guides, who shared in his mirth.

"I will take you for four hours. 1,000 riel each hour."

"I don't want to go for four hours."

And that was the truth. I did not want to spend the rest of my day on the back of an ancient motorcycle, no doubt being taken to different shops owned by cousins, uncles and other associates, all keen to sell me their wares, as part of the tour.

"OK. I will only pay 2,000. Where will you take me for that?"

After a few moments of thought he replied,

"OK. I take you to Wat Phnom"

"I will pay you when we get back here"

"OK. OK. Get on, get on."

His enthusiasm to get me onto the bike so quickly suggested that I must have paid too much for his services, but the deal had been done.

My guide had much to learn from the tuk tuk drivers in Bangkok. He actually took me directly to the temple without any stops at tailors, gem stores, or any other businesses where he could have earned a potential commission by introducing my custom!

He then told me to take as much time as I wanted, and walked over and sat down in the shade with what appeared to be, a group of other motorcycle guides.

I was now standing at the location that had given the city its name!

Although there are slightly differing legends, the basic story is that during the fourteenth century a woman called Penh went down to the river and found a washed up tree trunk containing five statues of the Buddha, four of bronze and one of stone. Apparently Penh was both pious and wealthy, and arranged for the construction of a ninety foot high hill. At the summit, she built a temple to house the Buddha statues.

In the process of creating the hill for the temple, Penh also created the only hill in the area. The temple became known as Wat Phnom or "Hill Temple," and the surrounding town became known as Phnom Penh or "Hill of Penh."

I actually found the shaded, grassy park surrounding the Wat to be quite peaceful. Perhaps this was because it was mid-afternoon, during the hottest part of the day, and most of the hawkers who normally plied their trade in the area were now sheltering from the heat. The shade and greenery provided a complete contrast to the heat, bustle, and traffic of the rest of the city just outside the grounds of the Wat.

The park was dominated by the hill that had been constructed all those years ago, with the focal point being the curved, bell-like shape of the main stupa soaring above the rest of the buildings in the temple complex on the hill top. After walking around the knoll and seeing the temple from all possible angles (and politely refusing peddlers, kids selling bric-a-brac souvenirs, and an elephant ride), I purchased a drink and sat in the shade to collect my thoughts. The day had become extremely hot and that, combined with the experiences of the morning, had left me feeling rather tired.

So I decided to go back to my hotel.

However, once back at the hotel, I soon became bored. Although it was nice to cool down in the air-conditioned room, the television options were extremely limited. After an hour of watching an American and Cambodian double act hosting a program teaching Cambodians how to speak English, I had to leave the confines of my room and get outside again.

It was now late afternoon, and the heat from the sun was nowhere near as intense as it had been only a few hours earlier. I left the front gate of the hotel and waved at my new friends, the motorcycle guides, who smiled and waved back, and I decided to go for a walk.

It was not long before I found myself down by the riverside (the city sits at the confluence of the Tonle Sap, Bassac, and Mekong Rivers). I decided to walk along the riverside esplanade in the Sisowath Quay district. The sun was visibly lower in the sky; soon it would be setting. With the end of the day approaching, the cafes, restaurants, and bars lining the esplanade were beginning to fill with a mixture of expats, tourists, and wealthier Cambodians, all out to enjoy their evening.

While I was sitting up on the riverside wall people watching, I noticed a small commotion up the road. As it moved closer towards me, I stood up to watch, transfixed. It was the elephant from Wat Phnom walking down the road! Apparently Sambo, as she was called, passed this way every evening with her handler on their way home. They made relatively slow progress down the road, as the owners of the various restaurants and cafes rushed out to offer Sambo food. She seemed happy to accept all offerings!

Once Sambo had disappeared down the road, the sun had set and I was feeling hungry.

Some of the restaurants in this area are famous for selling "Happy Pizza," which with its added herbs had a certain novelty value that made it popular with tourists. However, I bypassed these and entered a place that looked like it served more traditional dishes.

The owner asked whether I would like to sit outside or inside. Given how nice the evening was, there was really only one choice.

"OK. But don't give money or food to the beggars."

Since dusk had fallen, I had noticed a lot of amputees gathering on the streets. There are some 40,000 amputees in Cambodia. Most of these amputees are victims of landmines; a legacy of decades of war. Even when I was there, decades after the end of the conflict, an estimated twenty per cent of villages were still contaminated with landmines, with agricultural workers particularly at risk. Although casualty rates have been declining as more of the country is cleared of mines, there are still huge numbers of people who are unable to work due to loss of limbs, and who are consequently reduced to begging.

As I sat down the owner asked,

"Would you like the western menu or the Cambodian menu?"

I remember the first time that I was asked whether I wanted a local or a western menu, I was in Thailand and was quite surprised by the question. However, I soon discovered that this was relatively common in more touristy areas.

"I would like the Cambodian menu, but do not know what to order. What do you suggest?"

The owner's face brightened up.

"We have many Cambodian dishes. What do you like?"

Feeling the beginnings of a circular argument, I said,

"I like all types of food. Please, what is your favorite dish?"

"Amok Trei is our special dish."

"Excellent! I'll have that!"

As the owner walked away, I realized I had absolutely no idea what I had ordered. I really had to stop being impulsive, and getting so carried away with the moment.

While I was waiting for my food to arrive, a steady stream of amputee beggars came up to the outdoor seating area of the restaurant. Surprisingly, few of them tried to beg directly from the customers, but instead waited patiently. The owner, on seeing an amputee at the front of his premises, would hurry into the restaurant and come back with food, which he would hand to the amputee, before waving the person away.

Whether he helped these people because it was good business or because he was being a good Buddhist by offering alms to the poor, was hard to tell. I guess it was a mixture of the two.

While I was contemplating this, my food turned up.

When it was placed in front of me, I was still none the wiser as to what I had ordered. It was presented as a parcel of food wrapped in a banana leaf. The waiter then opened the parcel and I was hit with the familiar waft of aromatics that I have come to associate with a lot of dishes from the region. Before me was a fish curry in a yellow-brown sauce.

The waiter spooned some boiled rice onto my plate and left me to it.

The fish was delicious, all the more, because I had not eaten since breakfast. It was not a particularly hot curry, just gently seasoned and spiced to provide flavors that complemented the fish. After finishing my meal, I sat back with my beer, just enjoying being outside and watching people as they walked along the riverside esplanade. For the first time that day, I started to relax.

After paying the check, I went for a walk along the riverfront. After a short distance, I arrived at the Foreign Correspondents' Club (also known as the "FCC"), standing in all its grandeur in a three-story colonial-style building overlooking the river. I had wanted to visit the FCC and thought that I might have missed my chance. I walked in for a night cap and was not disappointed; it was everything that I had expected it to be.

The crowd was a mixture of expats and tourists with a few Cambodians. The cream colored walls, ceiling fans, and dark wood bar all evoked the peak of the colonial era at the beginning of the twentieth century. I ordered an Angkor beer and walked out onto the terrace. I was a bit disappointed not to have arrived earlier so that I could admire the view across the river while it was still light. However, I did smile when I overheard a rather loud and obnoxious man lecture his female companion about how he could feel the history of the city in this place, and how journalists would have met in the bar and exchanged stories in an era when there was a greater sense of adventure.

At that point I had to walk away to avoid openly laughing. Like many things I had experienced that day, the FCC was not at all what it first appeared to be. Despite projecting an image of Cambodia's colonial past, in reality it was established during the (very) late twentieth century by an enterprising expat!

However, listening to that obnoxious bore seemed to round out what had been a very surreal day.

The following is a simplified recipe for Amok Trei, using ingredients that are relatively easy to find outside of South-East Asia. Although the recipe has been simplified, I think it still tastes pretty good. More authentic recipes would include galangal (a root that looks like ginger but tastes very different) and would involve cooking the fish in banana leaves.

The Hungry Traveller's Amok Trei – serves 4

Shopping List

600g (1 lb.) monkfish or cod fillets (or the fillet of any other firm fleshed white fish)

¼ cup coconut milk

¼ tsp. turmeric

¼ tsp. paprika

¼ tsp. curry powder

2 tsp. minced ginger

2 cloves of minced garlic

2 tbsp. thinly sliced fresh chili

2 tsp. fish sauce

2 tbsp. vegetable oil

½ cup sliced onion

Salt and black pepper for seasoning

Preparation
Step 1:

Cut the fish into large bite-sized pieces. Season with salt and pepper and set aside.

Step 2:

Prepare the marinade by mixing the coconut milk, turmeric, paprika, curry powder, ginger, garlic, chili and fish sauce.

Step 3:

Add the fish pieces to the marinade and gently fold it together until the fish is well coated with the marinade. Leave for 20 minutes.

Step 4:

Heat the oil in a fry pan over a medium-high heat. Add in the onions and cook until they are softened. Add the fish and cook until it is just cooked or even slightly under cooked (the fish will continue to cook once it is off the heat).

Step 5:

Serve with rice.

I have also seen alternative serving suggestions where the fish is spooned into lettuce leaves and is rolled up and eaten like a spring roll.

Postscript

It appears that despite surviving the last fifty years, Sambo the elephant has a fairly uncertain future, with moves afoot to ban her from the temple grounds because of complaints that she is disrupting traffic. There are also stories circulating that Sambo has become lame.

The Highs and Lows
of Bush Camping

Location: Eastern Africa

One of my first adult travel experiences was when I traveled overland through East Africa, from Nairobi in Kenya, to Harare in Zimbabwe. I chose East Africa as a destination because at the time I had only a little money, but even with my meager savings I could still afford a ten week overland safari.

Although what I had booked had cost significantly less than other available trips, I thought nothing of it. I was just excited that I could afford to go away!

At the tour induction I soon understood why this trip was so much cheaper than any of the others. I had known that there would be a lot of camping but I had assumed that it would be in campsites. Campsites that had facilities, such as showers, flushing toilets, and with a bit of luck, a bar. But no, we were told, in order to have a more authentic experience we would doing a lot of bush camping. We were assured that it would all be great fun. And we did not have to worry about being without facilities for too long either. The longest stretch of bush camping we would have would be *only* three nights! However, the best piece of news was left until the end. We would all be on a rota to cook breakfast and dinner on a campfire.

The next day we were waiting at the agreed pickup point when down the road came a red truck with a green tarpaulin for a roof. It came to a creaking halt. It was a converted MAN troop carrier and must have been at least thirty years old. It had an enormous clearance, with the bumper coming up to the height of my chest. The inside of the truck was fitted with old dirty bus seats bolted onto a raised, weather-beaten floor that contained a number of sunken hatches. Air conditioning was provided by rolling back the tarpaulin - provided you did not mind getting burned by the African sun. However, we quickly found that this was preferable to leaving the tarpaulin roof in place, and sweltering in the resultant greenhouse that was created.

Once we had set off, cleared the traffic of Nairobi, and were on the open (empty) road, it became quite clear why we would spend so many nights bush camping. The truck had a top speed of around forty miles per hour, yet we would be traveling between towns, cities, and, more importantly, campsites that were many hundreds of miles apart. However, there was something quite mellowing about traveling at that speed. You could sit back, relax, and see the landscape gradually unfolding in front of you. And at that speed there was the opportunity, if you had keen eyesight, to spot wildlife, such as the occasional giraffe.

However, the novelty quickly wore off as we were confronted with various delays. These included washed-out roads, detours to local mission hospitals because someone else on the trip had fallen ill with malaria, and being held up for hours at a border crossing because a corrupt immigration official, angry at not being bribed, decided to make life difficult for us. These delays would result in us having to travel by night to reach the next campsite, followed by the almost impossible task of trying to make camp in the dark.

During the day we would stop at small towns and villages to take on critical provisions. These included "clean" water if it was available (which we would boil later before storing it in the truck's water tank), fresh meat (which, unless we were in a larger town, would be limited to whatever animal had been recently slaughtered), and fresh vegetables (if any were available).

At least once a week we would pass through a major town or city. On these occasions we would pick up enormous bags of charcoal for our campfires, as well as stocking up on non-perishable staples such as potatoes, rice, carrots, onions, and cooking oil, and as much meat as we dared fit into the on-board fridge. However, this fridge did not really keep anything particularly cold and critically, any food items stored there were competing with space for beer.

The process of setting up camp quickly developed into a regular pattern.

The truck would pull up at a real or improvised campsite. One person would open the wooden floor hatch containing the two-person tents and throw them off the side of the truck. Another would go to the luggage bay and unload everyone's packs. The cooking team assigned for that night would untether the large cast-iron grill and a folding table from under the truck, grab the charcoal, and siphon some diesel from the truck's fuel tank. We would then pitch our tents (in pairs or alone, if one tent-buddy was on the cooking rota that night). The charcoal would be arranged into a mound, wetted with some diesel, and set alight. Diesel was the best accelerant: it was volatile enough to light with a match but not so much so (compared with say, gasoline), that it would burn off before the coals had caught alight.

Within fifteen minutes everyone would have finished pitching their tents, and the cooking crew had drawn the ingredients for the night's meal from the larder (yet another hatch in the floor of the truck) and had begun preparing the food which would be ready in an hour or so. If we were lucky enough not only to be in a campsite but in a campsite with a bar, those who were not on cooking duty would go off and have a beer. If we were bush camping we would divide up what beer was left in the on-board fridge.

However, this level of efficiency was only attained after a couple of months on the road. In the beginning, such a degree of unspoken organization and teamwork did not exist. People struggled to put up their tents (not helped by the fact that just about everyone had missing tent pegs), and tents leaked and flooded because the spacers between the tent and fly sheet were missing and trenches weren't being dug around the tents. As for cooking, everyone still thought they were in their kitchens at home, and struggled with the idea of trying to cook with only a single sharp knife, a wooden spoon, and a large cast iron pot! And that was at a campsite which at least had basic facilities. When bush camping in the middle of nowhere there were no facilities.

It did take a while to get used to bush camping. Taking along a shovel as I set out to do my morning ablutions was a new experience for me, and within a few weeks my quads had a strength that they had never had before. Further, after a couple of months of experiencing African toilets, a hole in the ground was definitely not the worst experience that I had! It was also during one of these solitary moments that I witnessed one of the most amazing sights. It occurred when in Zambia, where, from where I was "positioned," I spotted a family of three elephants grazing on some trees at the bottom of a gully.

Another thing that you had to get used to when bush camping was the potential rationing of water, and having to brush your teeth with only one or two mouthfuls of water. Therefore any sort of body wash, or washing of clothes was definitely out of the question – but I guess that when everyone stinks, it is less noticeable.

I did always struggle though with being sweaty and grimy for a couple of days on end. After all, Africa during the summer months is generally pretty hot!

However, the one thing that struck me most about bush camping was the silence and, if it was a cloudy night or a new moon, the darkness. At even the most basic of campsites there would be some level of lighting, whether it was in the toilet/shower block, an onsite bar, or from other groups camping. Also, at these campsites there was generally always some level of background noise. The darkness of the bush camps was an inconvenience at first, especially when we were still novice campers stumbling around trying to find things. Also, as a city kid I initially found the silence hard to get used to.

After a while though, these became the very things that I loved most about bush camping. I would often walk just a few hundred yards away from the rest of the camp, lie down on my back, and look up at the night sky. In perfect silence I would stare at the multitude of stars that were visible due to the lack of city lights and pollution. Apart from the beauty of it all, there was also something quite humbling about the experience. Looking out into the heavens just shows how insignificant we all are – not just as individuals, or even as a species, but as a planet.

I remember the last bush camp that we had. We had driven a few miles overland, off the main road between Bulawayo and Harare in Zimbabwe. We had finally traveled far enough south that we were no longer in tropical areas where we had to worry about unexpected downpours, and the risk of mosquitoes infecting us with malaria had diminished.

We had arrived in good time to make camp. I had decided that rather than pitch a tent and feel stifled, I would improvise and just roll out a groundsheet and my sleeping roll, and suspend my mosquito net above me from a tree branch. I spent the evening sitting around with a good friend whom I had met during the trip. With our backs up against the enormous wheels of the truck and with beers in hand, we discussed how we could turn all of our experiences over the last couple of months into a fairly amusing "survival" book. Although we were due to finish in Harare the next day, we both had a few days before flying out, and decided we would spend some of the time sketching out our ideas in more detail. We would then work on them separately until we could next meet up a few months later, when we planned to both be in the same city at the same time.

It was a perfect evening to reminisce. The area in which we had set up camp was in an opening that was semi-enclosed with a few trees growing out of the red earth. The combination of the haze from the hot day and the sparse clouds in the sky produced a sunset with the most amazing colors. As the sun started to dip behind the horizon it gave off a deep red-orange light, complementing the darker red of the earth. The distant streaks of cloud turned a pink-red color while the sky directly above us turned purple. It was a perfect end to the day.

Later that night I lay awake underneath my mosquito net. I was going to be literally sleeping under the stars! I kept looking at the stars for as long as I could before falling asleep, wondering how long it would be until I would again be lying back gazing up at a night sky with so many stars?

Sadly, in to answer that question, it is still yet to happen again.

The next morning we broke camp and drove into Harare around mid-afternoon - right into one of the first of a series of riots, by people taking to the streets in response to high inflation and food shortages. At this stage the target was Robert Mugabe's government as the cause of their problems, and we managed to drive literally through the middle of the riot. Although the truck was pelted with rocks and pieces of concrete, people jumped out the way of the truck once the driver floored the gas pedal.

Although we had been through cholera and plague outbreaks and had almost drowned in the Zambezi river, this attack was pretty unnerving, and as we holed up in a campsite just outside of the city. No one had any idea what exactly was going on or how much worse the safety situation might become. Foreigners being attacked and killed in campsites was not uncommon at that time in Africa. The army had been deployed at the airport and at least for now controlled the main access roads. I knew that there was a flight out that night, so I got to the airport, bribed an airline official, and flew out that night.

Once I was airborne, I suddenly felt incredibly sad at how abruptly everything had ended. I had barely had time to say goodbye to anyone, which was a shame after such a long time on the road together. I said to my friend that we would somehow catch up later about our book, but as has so often been the case with friendships formed during my travels, I never saw her again.

Maybe one day I will find my photos from the trip and they will bring back enough of my memories to write that book.

The following is my ever dependable one pot chicken stew. My preference is to use chicken, but any meat you can find at the market during the day will work. Adding whatever fresh vegetables you can get your hands on helps to break the monotony of eating the same root and canned vegetables day in, day out.

The Hungry Traveller's Bush Camp One Pot Cooking Special – serves 6

Shopping List

1 chicken

9 large potatoes (the hungrier the group, the more potatoes you use)

1 onion

1 carrot

Chicken stock cube

Cooking oil

2 cans of chopped tomatoes

Any other fresh vegetables you can find at the local market

Around 1 litre (4 cups) of clean/bottled water

Pepper or chili flakes for seasoning

Preparation

Step 1:

Light the fire. This should always be done first to allow sufficient time for the flames to die down and leave the intense, steady heat of the charcoal and embers.

Step 2:

Prepare the raw ingredients. Cut the chicken into eight parts: 2 breast portions, 2 wings, 2 thigh portions and 2 drumsticks. Dice the onion and carrot as finely as possible. Cut the potatoes into even sized pieces. Try crumble and dissolve the stock cube into a little clean water.

Step 3:

Once the fire is ready, spread out the coals and place the grill on the top of the fire. Be sure the coals have a gradient of varying thickness, so that there is a hot part and cooler part on the cooking grill.

Step 4:

Pour some oil into a large, heavy bottom pot. Once the oil is hot, add in the onion and carrot and once softened, add in the chicken pieces.

Step 5:

Allow the meat to brown and then transfer the pot to a cooler part of the fire. Add in the stock cube, tinned tomatoes, potato pieces and stir. Add in the seasoning. Pour in the water so that all the ingredients are properly covered and simmer until the meat and potatoes are cooked.

Another World

Location: Sapa, Vietnam

I had been in Vietnam for around three weeks when I boarded the train at Hanoi station for the overnight trip to Lao Cai, a town in the north west of Vietnam on the border with China. Although my tourist visa was about to run out, I had been told by a couple of backpackers whom I had met in Hanoi that trekking out to the hill tribe areas near Sapa in the remote north-west mountains of Vietnam was a must do experience.

At the time I had a whole lot of questions.

"How do I get there? Where do I stay? Where do I go to arrange the trek?"

The couple smiled back at me, with that semi-patronizing manner that people who think of themselves as *travelers* have, when talking to *tourists*.

"Just catch the train to Lao Cai and take it as it comes. Enjoy the adventure."

I gave them the benefit of the doubt that they were not *deliberately* trying to be patronizing, and asked,

"Were there any problems getting around with SARS, given that you were at the Chinese border?"

"Nah. There were no tourists getting in the way."

"What, were you the only tourists there?"

I got up and left, hoping that my petty back-handed comment had landed. I walked across to the hotel reception and spoke to the owner, who happened to be on desk duty.

"How do I get to Sapa and organize a trek to the hill tribe area?"

"You not like Hanoi? Why you want to leave?"

"Don't worry, I will return after Sapa."

"Oh. OK"

This seemed to satisfy the owner, who continued,

"You catch train to Lao Cai. At Lao Cai you get a minivan to Sapa. At Sapa all hotel can arrange trek and homestay. You get night train there and night train back."

She then pressed on, sensing an opportunity to make a sale:

"I will book train. You leave tomorrow night and come back after two nights. You stay here one night, then you get train to Ho Chi Minh City."

It appeared it was all settled, then!

I arrived in Lao Cai early the next morning. Lao Cai itself was a fairly nondescript, modern town, having being basically destroyed and rebuilt after the Chinese invasion of Vietnam during the late 1970s. Across from the train station there was a row of minivans, the drivers of which were all aggressively peddling for the business of ferrying tourists out to Sapa. Given the small number of tourists, it appeared that there were probably as many minivans as potential customers.

I was approached by a driver who promised to take me to Sapa and was happy to drive me from hotel to hotel until

I found somewhere I was happy to stay (no doubt he wanted to make sure he could get his commission for introducing my custom).

The trip up to Sapa was along a winding mountain road. The road was fairly narrow, with a sheer drop to the valley floor. However, the lush green vegetation and the wispy mist across the mountains made for a fairly scenic trip.

Sapa itself felt like a European alpine village. It is perched on the side of a fairly steep hill and is surrounded by mountains. When I first arrived, the clouds were at the same altitude as the village, shrouding the town in a thick mist. The mountain weather was quite mild and the cooler air felt refreshing, compared with the heat and humidity of Hanoi.

As it so happened, the first hotel I came to had good rooms at very reasonable prices, and they agreed to organize an overnight trek with a homestay and the services of a hill tribe guide. What's more, I would be able to leave in under two hours.

While I was waiting, the youths who worked as porters and domestic staff at the hotel decided to practice their English with me. I say youths, but at most, they were in their mid to late teens. They told me that there were very few visitors coming to the hotel in recent months because of the SARS outbreak. They also told me that they were studying for their TOEFL (Test of English as a Foreign Language) exams so that they could get jobs working directly with tourists. Despite the death stares the hotel owner was giving them, they wanted to know if I could help them with some tutorial questions. I agreed, and spent the next half hour feeling embarrassed at how little English grammar I knew.

Once they realized that I was of limited help to them, they invited me outside for a game of hacky sack. After about forty-five minutes of showing that my foot and eye co-ordination was as good as my knowledge of grammar, I was saved by the hotel owner calling me in because the guide had arrived.

I entered the hotel lobby, where there was a young girl wearing an indigo-dyed linen skirt, apron, loose-fitting leggings, and a cylindrical hat, the dress typical of the Black Hmong hill tribe. Even by Vietnamese standards she was diminutive she could not have been more than four and a half feet tall. I looked at the hotel owner, who introduced her to me as my guide. She would take me to her family's house, he said, where I would stay overnight and be fed dinner and breakfast, before being brought back to the hotel the next day.

He told me if that was OK, I was to wait outside and my guide would soon be with me. Despite feeling pretty uneasy about the situation, I agreed and walked out.

Ten minutes later my guide skipped down the stairs. She had taken off her leggings and was wearing sneakers and had stashed her hat for a Nike baseball cap. The sight of the new combined with the traditional did make me smile to myself.

As we walked down through the village, she started chatting away to me in perfect English. After a few minutes I had to ask,

"So, how old are you?"

"I am sixteen," she replied.

Well, that was about five or six years older than she appeared.

"So why do you wear the baseball cap and sneakers?"

"It is more comfortable for walking. I put it on after western tourists agree to use me as a guide. Otherwise, they might not hire me."

As we walked down the hill towards the end of the town, I noticed more Black Hmong women in their distinctive clothing walking up the road. Relative to the other women, my guide was of average height. They were bent down under the weight of the goods that they were carrying. As if reading my mind she said,

"Today is market day in the town."

Soon we were through the town, and after rounding a corner, the road gave way completely. Before us was the valley floor and the bright green of rice paddy fields for as far as the eye could see, enclosed on each side by mountains. Some of the lower slopes of the mountains were terraced and under cultivation. The sun was also breaking out through the mist. The water on the paddy fields, and on what appeared to be a small stream running through the valley floor, caught the light and glinted in the warming sunshine. The sight was postcard perfect, although the photos I took did absolutely no justice to the amazing vista.

"We walk along here."

"But there is no path?"

"That is why I am your guide"

Well, I couldn't argue with that logic.

Although the walk was relatively flat, I had not come properly prepared for the conditions, and found the going slow. The path was essentially half a foot wide at most, and consisted of the slippery embankment that divided each of the flooded paddy fields. As my guide light-footedly traversed our zigzagging course through the valley, I trudged through with my heavy boots, thankful that I did not slip and fall into one of the paddies.

However, the scenery was amazing. It was as if the modern age had not touched the area. Men were working the fields with ploughs dragged by water buffalo, and little wooden and earthen shacks were dotted across the landscape. Eventually we reached the end of the paddy fields, and after walking along a track for a short distance, came to a very small village. We stopped for lunch.

I was led into a smoky wooden lean-to which was some sort of village restaurant. It had an uneven earthen floor and a kitchen area with an open fire. Looking completely out of place, there were also two plastic tables and four plastic chairs which rocked on the uneven floor. I was told to take a seat and asked if I was hungry. I was definitely hungry. I had not eaten since the night before!

Within a few minutes a pile of vegetables with rice was put in front of me. I noticed that my guide was not eating.

"Aren't you eating?"

"I am OK"

I had heard this all before.

"You are my guide. I should buy you lunch."

"I don't really want to eat that."

"Well, order what you would like to eat"

As the words came out of my mouth, I internally winced. I had been burned by open-ended offers of generosity in the past.

"OK"

My guide left and came back a couple of minutes later with a packet of plain biscuits. She then started chatting about herself, and once the floodgates had opened she didn't stop. She explained how we were going to stay at her aunt's house, and that it had been specially built for guests less than a year earlier. Her aunt was a really good cook and would make a feast that night. She said she was really excited that she had gotten the last minute request for the trip because her boyfriend, who was also a guide, was working that day and would be there that night as well with his group. She said that she and her boyfriend had plans to go to Hanoi.

"Why do you want to go to Hanoi?"

I got the expected response: the excitement of being in a big city, how she and her boyfriend could get an apartment together, and that all they needed to do was save some more money.

"Won't you miss living with your family and the area you have grown up in? Being a guide is a very good job."

However, the romance of the big city had captured her, and it wouldn't have mattered what I said. She was a sweet girl and quite intelligent, and was no doubt a lot more mature than I had been at sixteen, but she still lacked the necessary cynicism that came with life experience, and so had that naivety of believing that her life in Hanoi was *definitely* going to be so much better.

Given that she had not traveled beyond Sapa, I had to respect her courage and fearlessness at being prepared to step out into the unknown. I briefly thought about what the stark reality of life for her in Hanoi would really be like. Although she could speak English quite well, she presumably had only had a very basic education – maybe she would get a break and get a job working with tourists, but she was not ethnically Vietnamese, so I don't know if that would have made things more difficult for her. Most likely she would end up with a factory job and live in a heavily industrialized part of the city. But this was her dream and it would not have been fair for me, as a complete stranger, to crush it.

Instead, my reply was,

"Make sure you save up enough money for a return trip home before you leave for Hanoi, in case you change your mind and want to come back home. Always keep that money safe and never spend it."

I am pretty sure she wasn't really listening to what I had to say.

At that point, I paid for lunch and we set off to cover the couple of hours of further walking to get to her aunt's house. Most of the walk was along a dirt track, and every half hour or so, we could come across small groups of women trying to sell their craft wares.

"You buy something from me?"

Ordinarily I am not a shopper, but I was also conscious of the fact that business must be pretty bad with the lack of tourists passing through in the last few months. The women tended to sell similar items: hemp clothing dyed indigo (although seeing how it turned their hands dark blue as they handled the clothes, it was clear that the dye was not colorfast), embroidered and beaded bags and purses, and silver metal jewelry – mostly bracelets and necklaces.

By the time I arrived at the homestay, I had bought ten bracelets!

The guide's aunt's house was unlike any other place I had seen during my day of trekking. It had clearly been constructed by skilled builders and was two stories tall! I was given the grand tour. Despite the outside area being paved with concrete, the ground floor of the building was compacted earth and consisted of two large rooms which appeared to be a family living area and a sleeping area. The upper story, which was reached by a wooden ladder, was more of a mezzanine and consisted of sleeping space and mattresses for about twenty people. This was where the guests stayed, and it appeared I had my choice of places to sleep!

I dumped my pack and climbed down the ladder, where I was then introduced to the family. The men were sitting on plastic chairs on the concrete outdoor area. While inside a wooden lean-to (which was the cooking area), I was introduced to my guide's aunt and (I presumed) her cousins, who were busy working away. I was offered a seat outside with the men while my guide helped the women inside.

It is not often that I feel awkward. But the group of three men just sat there. Fair enough that they did not speak to me; I am sure they could not speak English. But they didn't even speak to each other! After fifteen minutes I could take no more. I smiled and nodded at the men and decided to go for a walk.

The house was actually part of a relatively sizeable farm. There were pigs locked away in a completely enclosed wooden sty. As I walked past, I could hear them squealing as they rammed their bodies against the wooden sides of the sty. I could also see their eyes pressed up against the gaps in the wooden slats, which was really unnerving. It seemed rather cruel, but I was told later on that this was a necessary precaution because the pigs were clever, and would find a way to escape and get into the crops.

There were also a couple of terraced fields, but these were planted with corn rather than rice. I presumed it was too difficult to irrigate a paddy, given that the river was some distance down the bottom of a steep hill at the bottom of the property. I also noticed a power line, presumably connected to a generator in the fast-flowing river, which ran all the way up to the house (I would later discover that this powered three light bulbs and was the only electricity in the village). I also found the location of the squat toilet and a large, open cesspit.

After my walk I returned to the main house. The men were still sitting there in silence. I walked over to the women in the lean-to and asked if I could help with the cooking. My guide looked surprised, and said,

"But the men are outside."

"If I would be in the way, I will leave…"

After a short conversation with her aunt, and some giggling from the cousins I was told,

"No, it is OK. It is just funny, because it is not the man's job to cook!"

I smiled and entered the lean-to. If only they knew my world. I could imagine the reaction if I told my girlfriend that as a man, it was not my job to cook.

There was an open fire pit of burning charcoal which gave off a lot of heat, around which the women were gathered preparing the food. There was a chicken, some eggs, what appeared to be pork, and lots of vegetables. Although I was offered a tiny stool to sit on, but I just ended up with my knees underneath my chin. I found it easier to kneel as I chopped up the vegetables.

"My cousin says you are very big!"

"I cannot be the first western man she has ever seen?"

"Well, yes you are, up close! You are the first man to come in and help cook. She is not allowed to talk to the visitors."

The women chatted among themselves as the worked, which suited me fine, especially when I compared it with the silence of the men sitting outside.

After I had finished my chopping, I noticed my guide grating vegetables into a bowl and asked her what she was making.

"Spring rolls."

"Can I help?"

"OK"

She passed the bowl across and handed me an assortment of vegetables, which I grated into the bowl. Finally, I cracked in an egg and mixed everything by hand. Then came the tricky part of rolling them up. Using two plates balanced in the dirt, I placed out two pieces of overlapping rice paper, spooned out the filling and rolled the spring roll up as tightly as possible. I think that given the conditions I did a pretty reasonable job, despite the concerned looks that were quickly covered with polite smiles from the women around me.

Any further awkwardness was avoided as the other group arrived at the house. My guide jumped up and told me to come out and meet her boyfriend and the other guests. Outside was a youth, all of five feet in height, flanked by a blonde woman who was at least five foot ten, and a man with sandy hair who was about six foot three. Both looked slightly ill at ease, while their guide chatted with the men sitting outside, who in turn seemed to have stirred into life.

After some brief introductions, I found out that the couple was Dutch but they were not very talkative. My guide went back into the kitchen to finish off the cooking, and her boyfriend sat down with the men. He pulled up a chair and motioned for me to sit down; he seemed to completely ignore his charges. He then proceeded through the usual list of questions: where I was from, whether I was married, and how long had I been in Vietnam. It turned out that he was nineteen. After a while I had to ask,

"Aren't you worried about the Dutch people?"

They were sitting off to one side by themselves. He answered my question by rolling his eyes.

At that point dinner was ready. He showed me to a table and called the Dutch couple over as my guide laid out the food. There was enough food to feed at least ten people, but places at the table for only three.

"Aren't you going to eat?"

"We eat inside. When you finish I come back."

He patted me on the shoulder and walked back inside the house.

After five minutes with the Dutch couple, I could understand why he was happy to completely ignore them when he arrived at the house. After five minutes of trying to make some sort of polite conversation I gave up. They were the most boring people I had ever met!

Another half hour of eating in silence, and then my new friend stood at the door way of the house and called out,

"Finished?"

"Yes. Thank you."

I couldn't get the words out fast enough.

Moments later, my guide came out and cleared the table. Then her boyfriend walked out with a handful of shot glasses and a plastic bottle full of clear liquid – literally, hillbilly moonshine.

"Now is time to have party!"

He started to hand out shot glasses. The Dutch couple got up, mumbled an excuse, and went inside.

"This is going to be a small party,"

I said, looking at the glasses and two quarts of rocket fuel.

"No my other friends who are guides will be here soon."

And as if on cue, the boys turned up. There were four of them. All were in their late teens and all seemed to be up for a good time. Glasses were quickly passed around and filled. The sickly pungent aroma of rice whisky filled my nostrils.

My new found friend, who was clearly the ringleader of the group, raised his glass and said

"Cheers!"

"No, No, No!"

I called out, and then shouted,

"Một hai ba, yo!!!!"

I had been in Vietnam for over three weeks after all, and this was not my first time drinking rice whisky with locals. The boys repeated it:

"Một hai ba, yo!"

1-2-3, yo!

And with that we drained our glasses.

It wasn't the worst rice whisky I had drunk since being in Vietnam, but admittedly that wasn't a very high bar to clear.

The glasses were refilled and the process repeated until about five rounds had been downed. This was going to be a dangerous night, but I was pretty sure that as I was twice the size of my drinking companions, they would be well and truly under the table before me.

That was to be a fateful error in judgement.

Mercifully, the drinking did slow down. I had the boys in stitches with my attempts at speaking Vietnamese, but most of all they were interested to hear about where I was from, what it was like to live in a big city, and the places I had visited.

"Một hai ba, yo!"

"So, what is Hanoi like?"

"It is a very big, very busy city. It is impossible to even describe it, compared with here."

"I want to live there one day."

"Really? Why?"

I may have been drunk but still had the sense to play dumb.

"Because this place is nowhere. I meet people like you and I want to be in the city."

"Một hai ba, yo!"

When I heard it expressed like that, I could understand where he was coming from. I came there thinking how idyllic the area was and enjoying the tranquillity for a few days. These guys on the other hand, were young, and were always hearing stories from tourists about there being a bigger world out there, with high-rise buildings, cars, roads, streetlights, lots of people, TV, and heaps of entertainment. It is a pattern that I have seen repeated all around the world, the younger generation wanting to leave the countryside in search of a more exciting lifestyle in the city.

"Một hai ba, yo!"

The drinking kept going. One by one the "boys" started to drop out, shake hands with me, and leave. I can't remember too much of what was said, but I do remember that when the last of the bottle of moonshine was drained, it was just my guide's boyfriend and I who remained. He seemed pretty unaffected by how much he had drunk. I, on the other hand, was a complete mess.

It was pitch-black but he managed to guide me back to the house. Somehow I made it up the ladder to the guestroom, where I crashed on the nearest available bed.

The next morning I awoke with the most terrible hangover. I crawled down to breakfast, and even though it was pancakes with banana and chocolate sauce, I couldn't stomach the thought of eating. The Dutch couple wouldn't even say hello to me. No doubt our party had kept them awake.

However, the thing that annoyed me most was seeing my guide's boyfriend bounce in all smiles and full of chat and completely unaffected from the night before. I took a couple of ibuprofen tablets and drank almost four pints of water before I felt even remotely human enough to begin the trek back to my hotel.

My last minute trip out to the hill tribe areas was a great experience, and I am sure I saw a way of life that despite being unaltered for many generations, would soon move on as the modern world caught up with it. In fact, when I went trekking in the hill tribe areas of northern Thailand a couple of months later, I probably got my best insight into what the villages around Sapa would be like in twenty years' time: There were fields worked with modern machinery, modern-style houses with satellite dishes and the locals that we saw along the way were mostly wearing western clothing.

I guess it is easy to lament the loss of traditions and culture and, yes, I think it is a shame that traditional cultures are being eroded by the influences of modern society. However, after meeting my guide and her boyfriend, I can completely understand why they would want to leave behind an existence based on subsistence farming, and go explore the wider world that is out there.

After all, when we go traveling, aren't we doing the exact same thing? And even if we chose to say rooted to the area in which we grew up, how many of us would forsake modern conveniences such as electricity, running water, and "luxuries" such as television, in order to live a much harder life purely because it was traditional?

The following is my recipe for vegetarian spring rolls. The recipe is based on one that I was taught at a cooking school that I went to in Hoi An, an old picturesque fishing village, and a place you definitely must visit if you are in Vietnam.

The Hungry Traveller's Vegetarian Spring Rolls – makes 6 spring rolls

Shopping List

1 cup of vermicelli noodles (these are prepared by soaking in boiling water until they are soft and the washing them in cold water)

1 cup of grated taro

1 cup of grated choko

1 cup of finely sliced Chinese mushrooms

1 cup of thinly sliced green beans

1 cup of sliced onions

1 egg yolk

9 rice paper sheets

Cooking oil

Salt and pepper for seasoning

Preparation

Step 1:

Mix all of the ingredients in a bowl and season to taste.

Step 2:

Separate the rice paper sheets. Each spring roll will require 1 ½ rice paper sheets. Lay out the full size sheet and place the half sheet on top on the side closest to you.

Step 3:

Spoon a sixth of the mixture onto the rice paper where there is a double thickness. Roll the spring roll tucking in the edges of the paper as you roll.

Step 4:

Pour oil to a depth of around 2 cm (1 inch) in a fry pan over a high heat.

Step 5:

Once the oil is hot, the spring rolls can be cooked. To test whether the oil is hot enough, place the tip of wooden chopsticks into the oil. If the oil is hot, bubbles will form off the submerged portion of the chopsticks. Place the spring rolls in the pan so that the open flap from rolling the spring rolls in facing down in the pan. As the spring roll cooks, turn the rolls in the same direction as they were folded.

Step 6:

When the spring rolls are golden brown they are ready to eat.

The Evolution of Food

Location: My kitchen

This is a bit of a cheat story. It is about what was once my "signature dish," largely because for a long time it was the only thing I could cook, my Fettuccine Alfredo. However, what I most like about this dish, and I guess in particular about the actual Alfredo sauce, is how versatile it is, and how it has evolved over time as a result of the influences around me, the people whom I have met, and even some of the places I have visited.

I have included a version of the recipe at the end of this chapter.

Food purists will no doubt scoff that I could call my dish Fettuccine Alfredo. Even my basic sauce of roux (butter and flour), cream cheese, and parmesan cheese significantly differs from the original Fettuccine Alfredo, which was first served by a Roman restaurateur called Alfredo di Lelio and consisted of a sauce of butter with Parmigiano-Reggiano cheese. However, this dish is not widely known as *Alfredo* in Italy, but actually became popularized in the United States where it has evolved into something quite different.

In a similar way, my dish has evolved over time.

Even as a student, I never subscribed to the two-minute

noodle philosophy. Cooking and eating proper food was important and felt a lot more satisfying than boiling a kettle. It was also not that much more expensive than pre-packaged noodles. At the time my dish was probably far closer to the original recipe, consisting of butter, parmesan cheese, and fresh black pepper.

The other great advantage of the dish was that it was passable enough to serve to guests. In time, I also found that it was an inexpensive way to impress girls. Invariably they would find it romantic that instead of taking them out, I would cook for them on a date. And I thought I was just being *economical*! However, I evolved the romantic image over time by including candle light (so it was hard to see just what a hovel I lived in) and a bottle of cheap wine. In fact my dish was nameless until I cooked it for an American exchange student, who said she was excited to be eating Pasta Alfredo for the first time since leaving home.

"Sorry, what's that?"

I had honestly never heard the name before, and I thought I was pretty knowledgeable about all things pasta. She replied,

"It's like this. But I don't think yours has cream in it."

Well, at least from that moment my dish had a name.

The mention of cream also gave me an idea, and I experimented with cream cheese to give a "cheesier," yet lighter-tasting sauce than cream would do. This sauce could then be thickened with some flour and used to make macaroni and cheese and cauliflower with cheese sauce.

When I graduated, got a job, and could afford to buy meat, I added other enhancements to my sauce, such as bacon and mushrooms. I also found that the Fettuccine Alfredo went well as a side with a piece of broiled chicken (I would be quite disappointed to find out years later that Chicken Alfredo was already a popular dish in America because at the time, I thought I was quite a pioneering inventor).

There was a period after I had started working when my Alfredo sauce was used in any number of different ways, to really become my cooking staple and signature dish among my friends and family.

Then, like the prawn cocktail, beef stroganoff, and chicken Kiev, my overuse of the dish led to it becoming unpopular. At first, it started with comments and good natured gibes, and ended with a friend refusing an invitation if I was going to serve "that cheese sauce" again!

Sic transit gloria!

Not long after this I quit my job and went traveling which opened my eyes to a lot of new flavors, tastes, and recipes. I never cooked my Alfredo sauce again.

Well, that is not quite right.

About three or four months ago I found myself having to make cauliflower with cheese sauce and rediscovered my Alfredo sauce recipe. I have had Fettuccine Alfredo a few times since, and despite all the years, all the travel, and all the different foods I have had since the heyday of my Pasta Alfredo, I still liked it!

Since rediscovering my Alfredo sauce I have made further changes to the recipe. The following is my current recipe for Fettuccine Alfredo. The latest evolution of the sauce includes the addition of nutmeg, which is a tip I recently got from a friend and completely lifts the flavor of the sauce.

In the following version of the recipe, I have also added onions, bacon, and mushrooms to the basic cheese sauce. However, the sauce is fine on its own too, without these extras. As previously mentioned this dish is quite versatile, and basic variations to the cheese sauce goes really well with chicken, white fish or vegetables.

The Hungry Traveller's Fettuccine Alfredo – serves 6

Shopping List

450g (1 lb.) of fettuccine

1 ¼ cup chicken broth

4 tbsp. flour

5 tbsp. of cream cheese

3 tbsp. parmesan cheese

¼- ½ tsp. nutmeg (freshly grated)

1 small onion finely sliced

2 cloves of finely chopped garlic

½ cup sliced mushrooms

2 rashers of bacon (diced)

2 tbsp. butter

Ground black pepper to taste

Preparation

Step 1:

Put salted water onto boil. Once the water starts to boil add the pasta.

Step 2:

While the pasta is cooking, fry off the bacon in a medium

sized saucepan over a medium-high heat.

Step 3:

Turn the heat to medium and add the onion until it softens and then add the garlic.

Step 4:

Add the mushrooms and once cooked thoroughly, put the cooked ingredients into a bowl and place to one side.

Step 5:

Melt the butter in the saucepan and gradually add in the flour over a medium heat to form a roux. And the broth and heat until the mixture almost boils (but don't let it boil). Add cream cheese and stir into the mixture until it becomes creamy. The sauce will thicken as it heats through.

Step 6:

Turn to a low heat and add the parmesan cheese and nutmeg and stir.

Step 7:

Once all cheese has melted into the sauce, add back the cooked bacon/onion/mushroom/garlic and stir until all the ingredients are combined and heated through.

Step 8:

Add the cooked, drained pasta into the sauce and stir through.

Step 9:

Serve with cracked black pepper.

The Taverna

Location: Lesbos, Greece

Arguably the best place to eat reasonably priced food in Greece is at a taverna. Like any restaurant these can vary in quality, but by and large, if the taverna cooks fresh food, the food will most likely be very good. When in Greece, like most other places in the world, if you see an establishment full of local people, chances are that the food there will be of good quality.

The other thing is to never be put off if you cannot speak the local language. The golden rule of travel is to always learn a few introductory words and sayings in the language of the country you are visiting. It is amazing how far simply being able to say *hello*, *how are you, I cannot speak <insert language>, can you speak English, please,* and *thank you* will take you. Most guidebooks contain these basic phrases, and they are well worth memorizing.

I won't pretend, you will not be able to have a full conversation with anyone in their native tongue, but you will break the ice and people will then make an extra effort to understand you, even if they cannot speak a word of English. However most of the time, unless you really are a long way off the tourist trail, there will generally be someone on hand who can speak enough English to help you out.

Yet I digress.

Another piece of advice when eating at a taverna, is to ask the proprietor what dish they recommend or is their specialty. A lot of tavernas may have a fairly extensive menu, but many only do a handful of dishes really well.

I have eaten at a lot of tavernas in Greece, but one experience has stood out more than any other. It was at a small village on the Island of Lesbos (or Lesvos, if transliterated from Modern Greek). One of the largest Greek Islands, Lesbos is located in the north-eastern Aegean, across from the coast of Turkey. Despite being famous as the home of ouzo, the liquorice flavored, distilled alcoholic beverage, Lesbos does not lie on the main trail for Greek Island hopping tourists.

I was on the island visiting my girlfriend's extended family, who lived in a rural village near the Bay of Kaloni. After a day of walking along the streets of the village, it felt as if every other person there was some kind of relative, no matter how distant! After hours of shaking hands and kissing cheeks, the family patriarch decided to take us and his immediate family to the local taverna for dinner.

It was just a small gathering of ten people that descended on the taverna, whose owners had laid out a long trestle table in the outside courtyard. Once we were all seated, a waiter came around and spoke to the patriarch, who turned to me and gruffly asked,

"Do you drink ouzo?"

I froze. I could not stand the taste of aniseed. Fortunately, my girlfriend jumped in to partially save the situation.

"We don't drink ouzo. What else is there to drink?"

After an exchange in Greek with the waiter came the answer,

"Green beer. Red beer. Water with gas."

I thought it odd that there was no wine option, but I guess this was the island of ouzo. So basically the choice was Heineken beer with its green label, Amstel beer with its red label, and sparkling water.

"Red beer, please"

When the drinks arrived, I really felt like the odd one out. Although a few of the women had opted for sparkling water, all the men were drinking ouzo. I gulped half my beer. It was a very warm August night.

In the meantime only half the ouzo drinkers had had their drinks poured out. An argument had broken out, and there were raised voices and much gesticulation.

"What's wrong?"

I whispered as subtly as I could to my girlfriend, who seemed oblivious to the commotion.

"Oh it's nothing!"

She replied. She continued to ignore me, but started to listen in on the "conversation" for a few minutes. Then remembering our "discussion" from the night before about not translating conversations for me just because she didn't find them "interesting," she sighed deeply and added,

"My cousin put ice in his glass before the ouzo was poured. My uncle is refusing to pour ouzo into his glass because he believes the ice should be added second. They are now arguing about whether ouzo is better with the ice added first or whether it should be added second."

"Does it really matter?"

But at this point my girlfriend had turned away to resume her conversation elsewhere across the table. For the next five minutes the argument continued with much hand waving and gesturing by the cousin towards his glass. Eventually, the younger man yielded and threw out the ice into a nearby plant. His glass was filled. Ice and then a little water were added, turning the clear liquid a cloudy white color. Finally, everyone raised their glasses.

"Yamas!"

There was a clinking of glasses around the table. After the second round of ouzo, the food arrived. As the different plates of *meze* were laid out on the table, the patriarch caught the arm of the waiter carrying one of the dishes, and motioned him towards me. He then announced in his heavily accented English,

"This dish is Sardele Pastes and is the specialty of the island."

At that point a plate of raw sardines – admittedly sardines with their skin peeled off, but still raw sardines, was placed in front of me.

"These sardines are the best in the world and caught from the bay. Enjoy them!"

He waved his hand off into the distance, presumably towards the bay.

I lifted two of the sardines onto my plate and squeezed on some lemon. I ate one. To be honest, I was completely underwhelmed

"So, you like them?"

I had just realized that everyone around the table was watching me eat.

"Very nice."

Well, what else was I going to say! Besides my reply seemed to do the trick and everyone had gone back to ignoring me. I nudged my girlfriend.

"What now?" she demanded.

I smiled sweetly to diffuse her annoyance towards me and asked,

"Isn't anybody else going to eat these delicacies?"

"No one else likes them!"

And she turned away again to continue her conversation. It is not often that I am speechless, but that entire episode completely threw me. I then looked around the table at the far more tasty dishes that had been laid out. The rest thankfully, were the standard meze dishes that I enjoyed, and the staple dishes that you can order in almost any half-decent taverna in Greece, and not be disappointed.

For the uninitiated, my favorite dishes (which you can never go really go wrong with ordering) include the following:

Salata
Greek salad: there may be a few regional variations to this but it basically includes tomatoes, cucumber, black olives, and feta cheese.

Potates
This will generally be handmade fries or fried potato slices

and is often seasoned with oregano.

Tzatziki
There are a few variations to this, but it is basically a Greek yogurt and garlic dip. It can often include shredded cucumber and sometimes mint and lemon juice.

Cheese Saganaki
This is a hard white cheese such as kefalograviera, pan-seared in a sagani, a traditional two-handled pan.

Louloudia
These are zucchini flowers, stuffed with feta cheese and shallow-fried.

Keftedes
These are meatballs (generally lamb) often served in a tomato sauce.

Tigantes miltzanes
This is fried eggplant.

Kalamari
Calamari (squid rings and tentacles dusted in flour and fried).

Oktapodi
Grilled or barbequed octopus.

Pita
Greek flatbread.

Eating meze is a great way to eat Greek food, as it allows you to sample a lot of different tastes by sharing dishes with your fellow diners. The food that night did not disappoint either, and with the amount of ouzo that was flowing, everyone was very merry by the end of the night.

Although I have eaten at a lot of tavernas in Greece, this particular meal stood out for me. This was due to a number of factors. The taverna was in a rural village serving authentic "old school" food, which tasted great and was made with fresh, good quality local ingredients. Also, it was fascinating to see so many people crowded around the table, picking at the dishes and talking passionately about the food – after all, there was a serious stand off about the proper way to serve ouzo!

But what do I remember most about that night?

It was when the check was presented in drachma (with a bracketed amount at the bottom in Euros), despite the fact that the Euro had been in circulation for over five years!

The following recipe is for cheese saganaki. Although simple to prepare, it is one of my favorite dishes (probably because I love to eat cheese). Traditionally, the dish is cooked in a sagani, but a small heavy-bottomed frying pan will suffice.

The Hungry Traveller's Cheese Saganaki – serves 6

Shopping List
450g (1 lb.) of kefalograviera cheese
1 to 2 tbsp. olive oil
Flour (for coating the cheese)
Lemons

Preparation
Step 1:
Cut the cheese into wedges.

Step 2:
Moisten the cheese with a little water and coat the cheese pieces flour.

Step 3:
Heat the olive oil over a medium-high heat.

Step 4:
Once the oil is hot, sear each piece of cheese until both sides are golden-brown.

Step 5:
Squeeze in the juice of a couple of lemons.

Step 6:
Serve while the cheese is still hot with pita bread and a glass of dry white wine.

A Tale of Two Cheesesteaks

Location: New York City and Philadelphia, USA

When I am in the north-east of the USA, one of my favorite foods is a Philly Steak Sandwich (or a cheesesteak if I am in Philadelphia). Whether it is served in diners, restaurants, or street stalls, a Philly Steak Sandwich is good, simple food that is hard to beat.

Although I have eaten lots of variations on the theme, all good cheesesteaks have the following in common: thin slices of fried beef, fried onions, and cheese, crammed into a long bread roll. They should also retain all of their meat juice and grease, which soaks into the bread. Variations to the above tend to be based on the type of bread roll used and "extras" such as sautéed mushrooms or bell peppers.

I always feel nervous discussing my experiences with foods that are considered iconic (let alone providing my own recipes for them), and writing about Philly Steak Sandwiches ranks right up there with talking about my favorite pizza experiences in Naples or the best Key lime pie you could eat in the Florida Keys.

Although I have had a lot of cheesesteaks, I am definitely not brave enough to publicly judge the best, but rather, would like to relate two very different experiences that I had involving Philly Steak Sandwiches.

The first was on a late spring day in New York City. I had been doing the tourist thing around Times Square, and decided to just follow my nose and go for a walk. After walking for a couple of blocks on what was becoming a warm day, I came across Bryant Park. The guidebooks make much of Central Park for obvious reasons, but for me the precious few acres of lawn and gardens that make up Bryant Park create a much needed oasis among the tall buildings and bustle of midtown New York.

When I approached the park, the tranquil sight of the shaded green space provided such a contrast to the hot, sunny, humid weather and noise on 42nd Street, that I was drawn towards it. The canopy of the large, mature trees that bordered the park created a soft green light in the shaded areas. However, what really surprised me was that in such a public space, there were moveable green chairs and tables and a bookstand. Given the reputation of big cities, I was amazed that none of this had been "lifted."

I picked up a newspaper dragged a chair around so that I was facing the lawn and could look out across the park as I casually flicked through the paper. It was almost as if I was reading the Sunday paper in my backyard at home! And I guess for people living in apartments in Manhattan, places like Bryant Park do become your backyard.

After an hour or so of reading and people watching, it was well into lunchtime and the lawn area of the park had filled with office workers enjoying a break away from their desks. I was starting to feel hungry too. Although there were a few kiosks, I did not want to run the risk of losing my table and chair. But then at the far end of the park I noticed a restaurant with what appeared to be a casual-looking, upstairs outdoor dining area that overlooked the park. Perfect!

I walked across to the restaurant. It was about half full of diners who all looked like city types. I was met at the door by the waiter.

"Perhaps you would prefer to dine upstairs at our outdoor café?"

I hadn't even opened my mouth. I may have been attired in *shabby chic* for a day of sightseeing, but being barred from a restaurant based on appearance was still a first for me. He could at least have lied and said that they were fully booked! However, I actually wanted to have lunch on the outdoor terrace, so I followed the waiter's directions to the stairs around the side of the building, and tried not to feel too slighted by the experience.

I sat at a table right near the terrace railing so I could look over the park. It really felt like a perfect day.

I scanned the menu, but there was only one thing that I wanted, the Philly Steak Sandwich!

After placing my order, I looked out across the park at the people dragging around tables and chairs or sitting on the grass eating their sandwiches. It all seemed so civilized. It was hard to imagine that during the 1970s this park was the complete opposite. Frequented by drug dealers, prostitutes and the homeless, the park had become a no-go zone. During the 1980s there was a regeneration scheme that eventually saw the park closed for four years, before it was reopened in its current form during the early 1990s. In many ways the park is symbolic of the renaissance of New York City at the time.

My Philly Steak Sandwich arrived with a knife and fork. To eat a cheesesteak with silverware, regardless of the venue, is sacrilege (the same principle also applies to hamburgers, as far as I am concerned). If a place is going to look down on me for eating a sandwich with my fingers, then they shouldn't serve it on their menu. However as a compromise, and in recognition of my surroundings, I did cut my sandwich in half before I started eating it.

What was served to me was perhaps the most upmarket cheesesteak that I have eaten. Served on a toasted ciabatta roll, it was piled high with thin slices of steak, fried onion and bell peppers, and topped with provolone cheese. It could have been perhaps a little bit greasier, but it was the first cheesesteak that I had in a couple of years, so it still tasted pretty good. It was also memorable because of the amazing, unexpected surroundings that I had stumbled across, by just randomly walking around the city.

My second memorable cheesesteak experience perhaps stood in as a great a contrast in terms of location as you could get. It was also the only genuine cheesesteak that I ever had because I was actually in Philadelphia!

I had a friend from my student days who lived an hour or so away from the city, so I agreed to swing across from New York to meet up one evening and catch up on the previous five years or so. As we both believed we could drink as if we were still students, we skipped any pretense of having a meal and went straight to a Belgian bar that he recommended.

Belgian beer, for the uninitiated has two things going

for it. It is generally a lot better tasting than your average domestic draft beer, so it is highly drinkable. It also has a much higher alcohol content than most domestic beers (Belgian beer can generally be at least twice as strong). This is a potent combination.

My friend and I were at the Belgian bar until it closed around five hours later. To be honest, I cannot remember too much of what we talked about, but I do remember that after that we went to an Irish-themed bar for a couple of hours until it too closed. It was there that I had my first Irish Car Bomb (the one and the same drink that I described in my previous story about Ireland).

When we were finally turned out onto the streets in the early hours into the cool autumn air, we were feeling very hungry. But in Philadelphia, you do not get a kebab in the early hours of the morning, you get a cheesesteak!

The cheesesteak stand was planted on the grass verge along a busy road, where people were literally pulling up by the side of the road to buy a sandwich. Around the stand stood small groups of people bundled up against the cold, scoffing down their food. They were all leaning slightly forward from the hips to avoid spilling any food on their clothing.

There was literally only one thing that could be ordered at the stall. It was operated by two guys who were working feverishly to keep up with the demand. Behind a glass counter, one man was dedicated to frying up the onions and slices of steak on a large, greasy grill. Using only two spatulas, he alternated between tossing the onions to stop them burning, and dicing the steak into even finer pieces while it browned on the grill. Once a batch of meat and onions was cooked, he would scrape it across to the cooler side of the grill, where the second man working on the stand would scoop it up into a long, crusty roll and *ladle* molten cheese over the top of the steak and onions, before handing it across to a waiting customer.

I have to admit that seeing melted processed cheese being poured onto a sandwich was a new sight. My friend, who saw me instinctively making a face, assured me that not only was it normal, it was the very ingredient that made a cheesesteak, a cheesesteak.

I was far too hungry to argue. The sandwich was messy and greasy, but above all, it was really good! Despite the cold, and the fact I was eating by the side of a busy road, I chomped my way through two of those sandwiches. My first experience of eating genuine cheesesteaks from Philadelphia!

As I mentioned earlier, there seem to be a multitude of variations to this iconic sandwich, which was invented during the early 1930s. Although the topic of what makes a perfect cheesesteak invokes a lot of passion from some aficionados, I believe that my recipe captures the essence of what makes a Philly Steak Sandwich so unique.

However, there are a couple of pointers that I have picked up along the way. It is important to use a decent cut of meat for the sandwich and to not skimp on quality. Rib eye appears to be the cut of choice and does have a good fat content, which helps make the fried steak pieces really juicy. Likewise it is important to use good quality, crusty bread rolls.

Personally, though, I think the emphasis on quality falls away a little bit with the use of processed cheese. I realize that the advantage of processed cheese is that you can melt it and pour it all over to properly cover the beef and onions, but as a matter of personal preference, I use Provolone cheese.

The Hungry Traveller's Philly Steak Sandwich (cheesesteak) – serves 2

Shopping List

250g (0.6 lb.) thinly sliced rib eye steak

2 tbsp. vegetable oil

Cheese – traditionally, the choices are Cheez Whiz, American cheese or Provolone

2 large long bread rolls or French baguette

1 sliced onion

1 sliced bell pepper

½ cup of sliced mushrooms

Salt and pepper for seasoning

Preparation

Step 1:

Heat an iron skillet or a non-stick pan over medium heat.

Step 2:

Add the vegetable oil to the pan and sauté the onions, mushrooms and bell peppers.

Step 3:

Remove the sautéed vegetables from the pan and set to one side.

Step 4:

Sauté the slices of meat quickly on a high heat.

Step 5:

While the meat is cooking, melt the Cheez Whiz in a microwave or place the cheese slices over the cooking meat to allow it to melt.

Step 6:

Once the meat is cooked, place the meat into the bread rolls. Add the onions, mushrooms and bell peppers and cheese.

Step 7:

Add salt and pepper to taste.

The Bridge on the River Kwai

Location: Kanchanaburi, Thailand

I remember watching *The Bridge on the River Kwai* growing up. This classic movie is based on the novel written by Pierre Boulle, about the construction of a bridge over the River Kwai by Allied prisoners of war, as part of the "Death Railway" during World War II. There were a number of things that I always remembered from the movie as a kid. There was William Holden's character, who escaped from the prison camp only to return as part of a commando mission to try to destroy the bridge. There was Alec Guinness's character, a stereotypical caricature of a British officer, who, with his stiff upper lip, defied the Japanese commandant on the basis that under the Geneva Convention captured officers should not be subjected to forced labor, but who then completely flipped his viewpoint and drove his men to build the best bridge possible (even to the point of almost foiling the attempt blow it up in the final scene). I also remember the Japanese commandant's famous quote about why he despised the British:

"You are defeated but you have no shame. You are stubborn but you have no pride. You endure but you have no courage."

However, what I remember most clearly was the theme tune for the movie, with the POWs at the end marching in step and whistling the "Colonel Bogey March."

However, when I got older and studied the history of World War II, my view of the movie started to change.

The Burma-Siam railway, or the notorious "Death Railway," was constructed between 1942 and 1943. Starting at a junction of the existing Bangkok to Singapore railway, it headed northwest to Kanchanburi where it crossed the river and continued through to the Three Pagodas Pass into Burma (Myanmar). In total, the railway line was some 260 miles long.

The construction of the railway was of strategic importance to the imperial Japanese army as it was used to transport men and supplies to the Burmese front, where the Japanese were fighting the Allied forces. The route selected by the Japanese army engineers traversed deep valleys and hills, but as earth-moving equipment was not available, all heavy work had to be done manually. As a result, thousands of forced laborers were used to construct the railway line.

Civilian forced labor was used to construct the section of line from Nong Pla Duk to Kanchanaburi, and Allied prisoners of war for the section from Kanchanaburi to Burma. The Death Railway is infamous because of the staggering number of deaths during its construction. Around 13,000 out of a total of 60,000 prisoners of war died. No records of civilian deaths were kept, but of the 270,000 civilians believed to have been involved in the project, it is estimated that between 80,000 and 100,000 perished.

Prisoners were subjected to severe conditions including squalor, brutality, and near starvation, which directly contributed to the horrendous number of deaths. The prisoners worked from dawn until after dark, and often had to march many miles through the jungle to return to base camp. The casualty rate among the POWs would have even been higher if it had not been for the efforts of Allied doctors, who tried to tend to the injured and diseased despite having no real medical supplies.

The section of the line built by the Allied POWs have become infamous through their association with the atrocities and hardships that were endured, and bear names such as the Pack of Cards Bridge, Hellfire Pass (Konyu Cutting), and the Wampo Viaduct.

When I traveled to Thailand, therefore, I felt that it was really important to visit the Death Railway and see the remnants of the true story behind *The Bridge on the River Kwai.*

Passenger trains still run from Bangkok to Nam Tok along the original route of the Death Railway. However after the war, the section of track from NamTok into Burma was removed because it was deemed unsafe and politically undesirable to maintain. However, what remains of the line still crosses the river near the town of Kanchanaburi.

I caught the ferry along the Chao Phraya River that runs through Bangkok, and across to the rarely ventured to west bank, to catch the early train to Kanchanaburi from Bangkok's Thonburi station. I wanted to get to the station well before the scheduled departure of the train because only third class tickets were available. This meant that there were no allocated seats, no fans, and definitely no air-conditioning. I definitely had to make sure that I got a window seat for the approximately three hour trip so that I could get the full benefit of the draft from the open window and watch the countryside roll past.

The train was not particularly full when it left. What was more surprising was how few western tourists were on board. The trip there was pleasant enough; if it hadn't been for the hot air blasting in my face no doubt the rhythmic *clickety clack* and rocking of the carriage would have lulled me to sleep - although I am sure that the stream of hawkers moving through the train selling drinks and food would have made certain that any rest that I did get was short-lived.

After an hour or so, I bought some pineapple from a hawker. As I licked the sweet sticky juice from my fingers, I started to think about the place I was going to and what I was hoping to find and understand.

Not long after studying the construction of the Death Railway at school, I found myself watching *The Bridge on the River Kwai* through different eyes and feeling quite annoyed at what I saw. Seeing Alec Guinness's character as almost collaborating with the Japanese was simply inaccurate, as the POWs actively sought methods to sabotage and undermine the structures that they built. The actual senior Allied officer involved with the bridge, Lieutenant Colonel Toosey, did as much as possible to delay the building of the bridge. Unlike Alec Guinness's character, Toosey encouraged acts of sabotage such as collecting termites to eat the wooden structures, and mixing concrete badly.

Furthermore, it is believed by many, that if a senior officer was seen as collaborating with the Japanese, the other prisoners would have taken steps to eliminate him.

In my opinion, the severity of the conditions that were endured was also underplayed in the movie. The savagery that was experienced cannot be overstated. The combination of exhaustion from overwork, starvation, beatings, and disease, reduced men to living skeletons waiting to die. Apparently, to end up in the hospital was tantamount to a death sentence, as the Japanese did not "waste" resources such as food on the infirm.

I also found it disappointing that where other movies such as *The Great Escape* portrayed the POWs as heroic figures defiantly standing up to their captors as best they could, the same level of reverence was not accorded to the POWs who worked on the Death Railway.

As the train pulled into Kanchanaburi station and I prepared to alight, I was still unsure of the question that I was trying to answer. Why did the movie upset me so much? It was not the first historically inaccurate movie I had ever seen. Maybe it was more of a demon inside me that I had put to rest?

I stepped off the train down to the platform. Leaving the station, I walked across the road to Don-Rak, or the Kanchanaburi War Cemetery. The cemetery is located a short distance from the site of the base camp through which most of the prisoners passed on their way to other camps.

During the war, the dead were normally buried near where they perished. However, with the creation of this cemetery after the war, the remains of almost 7,000 prisoners of war, who lost their lives during the construction of the Death Railway, were collectively reburied here.

A visit to a war cemetery is always somber and thought provoking, and Don-Rak is no different. Standing in the middle of the cemetery, all you can see are row and rows of ordered headstones, all perfectly aligned, stretching off in all directions. The perfectly manicured lawns between each of the headstones, gave the cemetery a tranquil, almost park-like quality. Walking along the lines of ordered graves you read the plaques. Each plaque represents one of the individuals who make up the harrowing statistics. The number of people who died starts to take on a more tangible quality when you see just how large a cemetery is required to hold 7,000 men, and then realize that this only represents a fraction of the total that died. And these were people, who did not die in combat, but from building a railway line.

Most of those buried here are from Australia, Britain, and Holland. All have died and been buried a long way from home and their grieving loved ones. Compared with the ages of those soldiers who are buried in World War I cemeteries, a number of the soldiers buried here could be considered "old," with a surprisingly large number in their late twenties and early thirties. However, all were struck down in their prime.

By the time I was ready to leave it was nearly midday. Despite it being so late in the day, I was surprised at how few people were at the cemetery.

Not wanting to walk for an hour in the heat, I caught a taxi down to the bridge.

I have said *the bridge* because in the original book that inspired the movie, Pierre Boulle just assumed that the bridge crossed the River Kwai because the Death Railway ran parallel with the River Kwai for a number of miles. However, the bridge actually crossed the much wider Mae Khlung, just north of its confluence with the River Kwai. However, these facts were not checked prior to the production of the movie.

After the film's phenomenal success though, tourists wanted to see the famous Bridge on the River Kwai. So in the 1960s, the Thais renamed the Mae Khlung the Kwae Yai, or Big Kwai. The original River Kwai was renamed Kwae Noi, or Little Kwai.

As you would expect, the wooden bridge in the movie, which crossed a fairly narrow river bed, is nothing like the concrete pylon and steel bridge that spans a fairly wide river. This is in fact the second of two bridges that were built by prisoners of war, with the permanent concrete and steel bridge having been built a few months after the temporary wooden one.

Given everything else that I have said about the movie, it probably comes as no great surprise to read that the destruction of the bridge as depicted in the film is entirely fictional. Both bridges were used for a couple of years, until they were eventually destroyed by Allied bombers. After the war the steel bridge was repaired, and is still in use today.

I was dropped off at the Kanchanaburi side of the bridge. There were a few more tourists around than at the war cemetery. This side of the bridge had been set up for tourism, with its own train station, and was surrounded by cafes and shops.

I walked towards the bridge. It was flanked on either side by replica bombs, and I noticed that people were walking across the bridge. In fact this seemed to be encouraged, as there were wooden planks placed across the sleepers and between the rails of the single track, to make passage easier.

The bridge itself looks like a fairly typical railway bridge, consisting of a series of steel spans resting on concrete pylons built into the river bed. The only thing that visually suggests something of the structure's past is that two of the steel spans are straight-sided, while the rest of them are curved. The straight-sided spans were added after the war to replace the spans that had been destroyed by bombing.

Between each of the spans are refuge bays, no doubt to protect tourists who happen to be on the bridge as a train is crossing.

Apart from the cafes and shops, one of the main attractions near the bridge is the JEATH Museum, an acronym for the main nations involved in the construction of the Death Railway (Japan, England, Australia/America, Thailand, and Holland).

I had heard much about this museum, famous for being built inside the grounds of a Buddhist temple, and for having an eclectic range of items on display. In part, the museum is constructed to recreate a POW camp. It includes a detention hut, complete with an elevated bamboo sleeping platform, on which photographs and physical memorabilia from the war are on display. There were also displays of abandoned equipment which was also quite interesting.

However in other areas, the fact that the museum was managed by enthusiastic amateurs was very apparent. The display showing the bridge being constructed, so that it looked like a section of track that stretched out over the actual river, was a good idea. However, the life-size plaster figures of the working prisoners were done so poorly that they looked almost comical. Likewise, in the display of the war leaders, the serious educational message being attempted was partly lost due to the very amateurish looking plaster statues.

None of this could prepare me though, for the section of the museum with the Miss Thailand posters. After reading accounts of the terrible conditions and suffering, and seeing photos of emaciated POWs, I couldn't decide whether this rather glib display was surreal, comical, embarrassing or insulting. Leaving the museum I felt a combination of all these emotions.

However, it was now getting towards late afternoon and time to check into the guesthouse where I was going to stay for the night. Back when I had booked the accommodation in Bangkok I had been instructed to wait near one of the cafes by the river for my transportation to the guesthouse. When I arrived I was greeted by a man who walked me along a track down to the river bank. Among the reeds, there was a small clearing and a bamboo raft. An older woman, who had been sitting on the raft got up as she saw us approach, picking up a long bamboo pole.

"Please. Jump across. She will take you by the raft to the guesthouse."

I stepped across from the muddy bank onto the raft.

"Sawadee-krab!"

I greeted the woman as I boarded. She gave a single nod and replied,

"Sawadee-kah."

I noticed the man was walking away.

"Isn't there anyone else coming?"

But he was already out of earshot.

The woman took a step towards a small raised platform in the middle of the raft and patting it with her hand, motioned for me to sit down. I did as I was told and with that she pushed off from the bank and guided the raft out into the river. We traveled along in silence, the current of the river sweeping us along at a fairly reasonable speed. Once the cafes and shops had been left behind it was extremely tranquil on the river, and there were few signs of human habitation along the bank. If it hadn't been for my guilt at sitting down while the older woman behind me guided the raft with the occasional grunt, I would have found the whole experience quite relaxing.

After around fifteen or twenty minutes we rounded a bend in the river, and a series of bamboo buildings sitting on pontoons came into sight. The woman guided the raft towards these buildings, moored it to one of the pontoons, and walked onto the landing, past the bamboo huts, and onto the grassy river bank. I assumed the guesthouse was nearby and followed her. Arranged around an open grassed area was a series of buildings. The woman pointed me towards one of the buildings, smiled and nodded, and walked off.

The site appeared completely deserted, as I walked towards what appeared to be the main building. I pushed open a door and entered a dining area decked out with plastic tables and chairs.

"Hello!" I called out.

There was no response, so after a few minutes I noisily

pulled out a chair and sat down. This had the desired response. A young woman walked into the room, let out what sounded like an "oh" and scampered out again. A few minutes later a woman who looked like she has just woken up walked in.

"Hello. You book for guesthouse tonight?"

I was beginning to wonder if I was at the right place.

"Yes. I just came down from the bridge on a raft."

"Ah. You early! It not busy, you can stay in floating hut."

With that she walked over to the other side of the room, unlocked a door to what appeared to be an office, and went in. A minute or two later she returned with a key attached to a large plastic bubble, and motioned me to follow her. As we walked across the grass yard she gave me a tour of the facilities; the tour consisted of standing in the middle of the yard, and shouting and pointing around her.

"Walk there to road. Turn left to walk to bridge. There toilet block. Over there shower. Behind is bar and dining room. In two hour will be open. We sell beer and food. Food very good. OK."

I wasn't sure if the OK was a question or a conclusion to the conversation. I replied "OK" but she had already started off towards the buildings on the floating pontoon. We had basically walked back around to where the raft was still moored. There was a thatched building with three doors leading to three separate rooms. She unlocked the middle door.

"This is where you stay tonight. Leave key in door when you leave. Have nice stay."

As she was on her way out, she stopped as if she had forgotten something and called back, "You on tour to Hellfire

Pass tomorrow. Truck pick you up on road outside at 9:30 a.m. Don't be late."

I stood dumbfounded, watching her retreating form until she rounded the corner of the building. I then stepped inside the door to the room. Basically everything had been constructed from bamboo: the floor, the frame of the building, the nightstand and the frame of the bed. The walls and roof were made of thatched bamboo fronds (I really hoped that there would not be heavy rain during the night). The only things that were not made of bamboo were the mattress and bedding, a mosquito net suspended from the ceiling, a single light bulb hanging from the central rafter, and a small rotating fan sitting on the nightstand.

I put down my small pack and stood in the doorway. The door to the room faced the river, and it was actually quite hypnotic watching the river flow past. I stepped back outside onto what could be best described as the porch area and leaned on the bamboo balcony railing, hoping that there would not be a storm that night, which would cause my little hut to break free of its moorings and end up smashed to pieces somewhere downstream while I slept.

As there was nothing more to do than enjoy the peace and quiet, I sat down with a book on the bamboo bench outside my front door and enjoyed a few hours of solitude.

Once the light had faded I gave up on reading. Besides, the mosquitoes were out. Happily the bar had been open for about an hour, so I locked my door and walked up to the main building.

The dining room/bar area was basically deserted. A

serving hatch that appeared to operate as the bar had opened up, and was staffed by the younger woman I had seen earlier in the day. I asked her for a beer. I looked around; there was only one other guy there, sitting by himself drinking a beer. The obvious thing to do was to walk over and introduce myself.

My drinking buddy was Dutch, and had come out to the area because while he was backpacking around Thailand he had remembered the Death Railway from school and decided to come and check it out. He had been staying there for five days now!

"What have you been doing here?"

"Just relaxing."

"Have you been across to the other side to see Hellfire Pass?"

"No."

"Have you caught the train across to the end of the line?"

"Um, no."

"So how have you been passing the time?"

"I have walked across the bridge a few times. That was pretty good."

He was a nice enough guy.

After about an hour the lady of the house came into the room. She spotted us and walked over.

"You going eat dinner now."

It was a statement rather than a question. She then turned to me.

"You like Thai green chicken curry?"

"Yes, I do."

"OK I get for you."

She then turned to the Dutch guy and said,

"Cheeseburger and chips for you."

And then she walked off.

About fifteen minutes later the younger girl returned with our food, and the owner with the check. The owner also handed the Dutch guy a squeeze bottle of mayonnaise, which he proceeded to pour all over his fries.

"Just like in *Pulp Fiction*!"

I quipped. However, this comment just drew blank looks, so I focused on the bowl in front of me.

The chicken curry had been ladled into the bowl on top of a layer of boiled rice. The food smelled great and was redolent of fragrant lemon grass and coriander. The coconut milk combined with the curry paste gave the sauce a pale green color. I tasted some with a spoonful of rice. Wow! It certainly had some kick! The owner wanted to know if I wanted some sugar to help reduce the intensity of the chilies, but I said that it would be OK. At this guesthouse in the middle of nowhere, I was eating probably the best green chicken curry that I had had since arriving in Thailand. The guy opposite me was eating what looked like a rubbery burger with soggy fries. The expression *when in Rome* came to mind.

The next morning I was squatting by the roadside more than fifteen minutes early for my tour out to Hellfire Pass. I had risen early, had a cold shower, and spent over an hour sitting outside my cabin, staring at the river flowing past me.

A truck came trundling down the road from the direction of the bridge and pulled up in front of me. From the driver's cab a voice called out,

"You here for Hellfire Pass trip?"

I nodded.

"Climb in back!"

I walked around to the back of the truck and climbed on up. The truck was already fairly full, and it seemed that I was the last pick up as we drove straight to the Hellfire Pass memorial.

Officially called the Konyu Cutting, this part of the Death Railway belongs to the section of the line that was lifted at the end of the war. The term *Hellfire Pass* was coined by the POWs because the sight of the emaciated prisoners laboring at night by the flickering light of oil lamps and wood fires resembled a scene from hell. The human toll in constructing just this section of the line alone was enormous. The work began in late April 1943 with 1,000 POWs. Many of these men were already sick but were still required to work eighteen hours a day. It took six weeks to complete the cutting through a depth of twenty yards of hard limestone. During this time, sixty-nine men had been beaten to death by guards and many more had died from disease, starvation, and exhaustion. In total, it is estimated that four hundred people died completing the pass. By mid-August 1943 there were only a hundred survivors.

After walking up to the stairs to the start of the cutting, I saw the rather poignant and moving memorial, which consisted of railway tracks running off and disappearing into the ground. As I walked along the disused track bed at the bottom of the cutting, it was possible to still see the cutting marks made by hand tools. In the heat and the still air of the day it was easy to imagine how so many suffered and died from exhaustion. What was hard to comprehend though, was the sheer number of POWs that had died over such a relatively short section of the line. The full meaning of the expression *a death for every sleeper*, which has been used to describe the Death Railway, started to become very clear.

Unfortunately there was insufficient time for me to walk the full distance of cleared track bed that would have also taken me past the locations of *Three Tier Bridge* and the *Pack of Cards Bridge,* and *Compressor Cutting,* and I had to climb back on board the truck to be driven to Nom Tok station to catch the train back to the River Kwai Bridge station.

I managed to get a seat by the window on the right-hand side of the carriage. This was the side of the train that ran alongside the original River Kwai. The view alongside the river was extremely scenic. However, as the train slowed to a crawl to cross the Wampo Viaduct my heart was in my mouth. Even though the trestles had been extensively rebuilt after the war, looking out of the carriage window at the expanse of trestles supporting the track over the sheer drop to the river valley below as the train slowly creaked along, was not for the faint hearted.

As the train approached the bridge that had been made famous by the movie, it slowed to a crawl and, with its horns blaring, proceeded across. I now understood why tourists were not routinely killed crossing the bridge on foot, given that it was just about possible to out walk the train. Even so, pockets of tourists had assembled themselves into the safety bays between the spans of the bridge and were waving madly at the train as it passed by like little kids.

I hopped off the train at the River Kwai Bridge Station.

I had decided to get a minibus back to Bangkok just in case the train journey had been an unpleasant experience, and I now had an hour to fill in. After walking around the shops for a bit I bought a coconut ice cream, which I soon discovered had the unnecessary additional ingredient of kernels of corn.

Eventually the minivan turned up, and after a cramped, sweaty half hour in a middle seat, I was regretting that I had not stayed on the train all the way back to Bangkok.

To try pass the next two and a half hours, I turned my mind back to why I had such strong feelings about the movie and my reasons for coming out to Kanchanaburi to visit the sights connected with the Death Railway. More importantly, had I managed to answer the questions I had when I had gotten off the train at Kanchanaburi station?

I think so.

When I was growing up, attendance at annual memorial services for the war dead was compulsory. Apart from the sounding of the Last Post, the other thing that I clearly remember was the constant repetition of *Lest We Forget*.

The generation who served in World War II was rapidly passing away, and the story, the first-hand accounts of what really happened during the war, was passing with them. I thought of my grandfather, who had fought for the entire six years and yet never spoke a word about it. When he died, all his stories and experiences died with him. From what I could gather a lot of his experiences were unpleasant, but it was still a piece of history that is now lost forever.

Maybe that is why I had such a problem with the movie. It was produced at a time when the real stories of what happened were still fresh, and it was relatively easy to find veterans to retell their experiences. In my opinion, what was produced instead was a factually weak movie based on a factually weak book. There was a squandered opportunity to have educated, as well as entertained. The fact that so many people will continue to watch the movie and accept the story as accurate is what saddens me when I think about the "real" stories and history behind the Death Railway.

However, the redeeming feature of the movie is that there will always be some people who will feel inspired to travel to Kanchanaburi, and that way will get a sense of the real achievements and the enormous human cost that was attached to them.

As a result of the trip, one of my favorite Thai dishes is green chicken curry. In my opinion, the following recipe makes a curry with a medium heat, but these things are very subjective! To weaken the heat of the curry, use less green chilies (or remove the seeds), when making the curry paste. Alternatively, add more coconut milk.

If you want to cheat, you can buy green curry paste rather than make your own. The recipe I have included is based on ingredients that should be readily available if you don't live in South East Asia or have access to a specialist grocer.

The Hungry Traveller's Thai Green Chicken Curry – serves 4

Shopping List

For the curry dish:

3 tsp. green curry paste (or to taste)

450g (1 lb.) chicken breast cut into large bite-sized pieces (alternatively, an equivalent weight of chicken thighs could be used)

400mL (1.65 cups) coconut milk

2 tsp. Thai fish sauce

1 tsp. palm sugar (or caster sugar)

3 tsp. vegetable oil

Salt and pepper for seasoning

Boiled rice

For the green curry paste:

10 whole green bird eye chilies (add more or less to adjust the heat of the dish)

2 lemon grass stalks

1 tbsp. ginger

½ tsp. roasted ground cumin

½ tsp. roasted ground coriander seeds

3 garlic cloves

5 spring onions

1 tsp. shrimp paste

4 limes, zested and juiced

3 handfuls of fresh coriander on the stalk

Preparation

Curry Paste:

The curry paste can be made in advance of cooking the curry.

Place the roughly chopped ingredients for the curry paste into a food processor or a liquidiser and blend until the ingredients form a paste.

Curry Dish:

Step 1:

In a large frying pan, heat the oil until it is hot.

Step 2:

Spoon in the curry paste and stir it around to begin the process of cooking out the spices.

Step 3:

Add in the chicken and seal the meat.

Step 4:

Pour in the coconut milk. When it comes to the boil stir in the fish sauce and sugar.

Step 5:

Turn the down the heat and simmer until the chicken is cooked.

Step 6:

Serve with boiled rice.

Cocktails, Sunset, and Key Lime Pie

Location: Florida, USA

There are times when you just need to get away. To leave the drudgery of your life behind and just do nothing. I guess that is what I call a vacation (as opposed to going somewhere to see and experience different things).

It doesn't happen that often to me. Deep down, I am actually a fairly positive and upbeat person, but I remember that I had just had enough. It was summer and yet my skin was pale from a combination of indifferent weather and being stuck behind a desk during most daylight hours (including weekends). Work was depressing. I felt as if I was just trudging along on a treadmill, waiting for something to happen. That something was probably going to be me hitting breaking point.

On an impulse, I took leave from work and booked a flight and rented a vacation rental overlooking the beach at Sand Key, on the Gulf of Mexico coastline in Florida, to try and unwind. The beach is actually located on an island, one of a number of so-called barrier islands, which can are reached by crossing one of the causeways or bridges linking them to the mainland.

As I drove across the causeway from the airport, I looked out at the blue expanse of water of the Intracoastal Waterway, glittering in the afternoon sunshine, and already felt the tension start to lift in my neck and shoulders. White boats were cruising along the still water. I felt envious of those people who had homes down by the water and could have this relaxing view right outside their windows.

By the time I had checked into apartment it was late afternoon. The sun was sitting lower in the sky and, through the west-facing windows, bathed the entire apartment in golden yellow light. I dropped my bag and instinctively let out a sigh. Walking towards the window, I touched the glass; despite the air-conditioning it was very warm to the touch. I grabbed a beer from the fridge and, after fumbling with the lock on the sliding door for a few minutes, walked onto the balcony.

Although it was still fairly hot, the evening sea breeze had started. My apartment was ten stories up and the balcony directly overlooked the white sandy beach below. There were sweeping views up and down the coast. The glare of the late afternoon sun on the water was too much for my eyes, so for the first time in over a year I put on my sunglasses. I dragged a chair towards the balcony, sat down, and put my feet up on the railing. I took a sip of the cool bitter liquid and closed my eyes, feeling the warmth of the air on my skin. All I could hear was the rhythmic rolling of the waves, gently breaking on the beach and washing back out. There was the occasional cry of a sea bird. I opened my eyes and watched the few remaining people on the beach pack up their towels, umbrellas, and beach chairs as sunset approached.

As the sun moved closer to the horizon the yellow glare diminished and the light softened, and its color became a light orange. As it slipped ever closer to the horizon, its light further diminished as it went a deeper and darker shade of orange. Eventually, the sun resembling an orb of burnt-orange, was swallowed up completely by the horizon. For a few more defiant minutes it threw out a few last beams of orange light that into the western sky, before being chased away by a sweeping band of purple that eventually turned black.

In the space of half an hour I was sitting in complete darkness. There was no moon. The sea, the sky and my apartment were all completely black. I drank the last of my beer and as I started to relax for the first time in so long, the exhaustion of the last year or so caught up with me. I walked into the bedroom and lay on the bed; although I had been traveling all day I was too tired to shower, too tired to change, and even too tired to get under the covers.

I slept for sixteen hours straight.

I eventually awoke the next day, as my eyes could no longer keep out the bright light that was streaming into the apartment. I stiffly got up and looked in the mirror. My face was creased from whatever it was I had been lying on – it hadn't been a soft pillow! My hair was greasy and plastered to my head, and my eyes had sunk into the recesses of my skull. My skin looked gray and my breath smelled like the bottom of a birdcage. I stumbled into the shower.

After a little bit of grooming, I at least looked human. I was starving and went out into the glaring sunlight and blazing heat of the early afternoon to buy some groceries and catch up on the last four meals that I had missed. Returning to the apartment, I didn't at all feel like going out, much less doing any sightseeing. Instead, I poured myself a tall, cold drink, grabbed the book that I had been meaning to read for over two years (but had never gotten around to starting), and sat on the balcony in the sun. With my legs dangling over the railing, I started to read.

The next thing I remember was jolting awake.

I had dropped my book after only reading a few pages. I had no idea how long I had been asleep, but my arm was red from the sun and judging by the sun in the sky, it was late afternoon. I stood up, leaned over the balcony, and breathed in the air, looking up and down along the coast. In the section of beach immediately in front of me, groups of kids were building sandcastles with their parents. I watched, transfixed, as one fairly creative woman crafted a sea turtle sand sculpture with no more than a bucket, water, and a trowel.

After about ten minutes I noticed one of the kids pointing out to sea and jumping up and down excitedly. His parents also started pointing as well. I looked out, and I could see it too! It was a pod of three dolphins, weaving in and out of the water, less than fifty yards from the shoreline. The dolphins did not seem to be in a rush to go anywhere, and appeared to be swimming in and out of the swell. For the first time in ages, I felt a smile on my face.

The serenity of the scene was suddenly broken by the guttural, pulsing roar of diesel engines as a large, bright yellow speed boat full of dolphin-spotting tourists came rushing over. As soon as the boat was within a few hundred yards, the dolphins swam out towards the deeper water, away from the boat, which circled around the area where the dolphins had last been seen before turning tail, and slowly cruising back up the coast, full of disappointed passengers. The throbbing of the engines could still be heard long after the boat was out of sight. I smiled sardonically. Served them right for coming in and scaring off the dolphins!

I sat back down and read for a little longer in the fading light, pausing only to watch the setting sun. Once it was too dark, I walked back into the apartment and for the first time in probably over ten years cooked some Fettuccine Alfredo. I had forgotten how much this was comfort food to me and ate three helpings! By then I was feeling tired, and went to bed.

This sedentary and rather solitary existence went on for quite a few days. After initially going red, my skin had started to darken, and I no longer looked gray. All that sleep had done wonders as well: I could see my eyes again in the mirror rather than two sunken dark recesses.

And then one afternoon, I felt bored with doing nothing but reading!

I was flicking through the usual assortment of tourist brochures looking for somewhere to go, when, I saw an ad for the Palm Pavilion Beachside Grill and Bar. It was located right on the beach, and claimed to be the place "where all the locals go." Most importantly, it had *Grill and Bar* in its name!

When I arrived at the Palm Pavilion, it was late afternoon and blisteringly hot. From the parking lot, the building appeared quite unassuming. Inside, there was an expanse of rough wooden flooring leading across to a bar that ran the length of the entire wall. Although this area could hold well over a couple of hundred people, it was empty apart from the wait staff; all the patrons were sitting at tables on the outside decked area. I was shown to a table. From where I was sitting, all that that separated me from the sandy beach was a low railing.

The original Palm Pavilion dates back to the 1920s, when it opened as a bathing pavilion. People arriving from the mainland by boat would rent space, where they could change into their beachwear. Over the years, the business branched out and started selling accessories, then snacks, before offering a lunchroom. Despite major renovations and expansion into its current form, I found the building to still be reminiscent of a 1920s bungalow.

Although the day was hot it was quite cool sitting outside, thanks to the large umbrella shading the table and a series of large fans blasting air in the direction of the customers. I ordered a house cocktail, sat back, and watched a kite-surfing class. All I can say, after watching the class of struggling beginners, is that kite surfing is definitely a lot harder than it looks.

The restaurant bar had quite a relaxed and casual feel, and was just what I needed. After all, I was at the beach on vacation! After enjoying a couple of cocktails and watching the rolling waves coming off the Gulf of Mexico while listening to the live band (who weren't half bad), I was soon feeling quite hungry.

I asked what the waitress what she recommended.

"Well if you are hungry, I'd go for the burger."

I was feeling hungry.

"Great! I'll have the burger then, with a side order of fries"

I was so hungry that I was ready to demolish anything put in front of me.

However, I was taken aback when I saw the enormity of the meal that was placed in front of me.

I honestly thought that the burger was the size of my head. And I have a big head! The smell of the grilled meat was heavenly, and the burger was delicious. I took my time, and ate the entire burger while watching the sunset. I even managed to eat half of my fries.

After clearing away my plates, the waitress returned

"Would you like to look at our desert menu?"

I said I couldn't even move, let alone eat anymore.

"Oh, but you have come so far to be here, you have to at least try our key lime pie. It is our specialty."

For those who do not know, key lime pie is named after the key lime, which is associated with the string of islands that lie off the southern Florida Coast known as the Florida Keys. The pie is similar to tarte au citron, but rather than using lemons it is made with key limes.

Although the pie is believed to have been invented in the late nineteenth century, the first recorded recipes date back to the 1930s, when the pie filling consisting of key lime juice, egg yolks, and sweetened condensed milk (as fresh milk was not widely available in the area at the time) was described. The addition of the lime juice to the egg and condensed milk mixture causes the filling to naturally thicken and "cook" due to the acidity of the lime, in a process called "souring."

Although an authentic key lime pie should be pale yellow in color (given that key lime juice is pale yellow) and have a pleasant tangy flavor, the several times I had previously had key lime pie (admittedly not in Florida), the filling had been bright green and overly tart, resulting in an unpleasant experience overall.

However, I put aside my natural trepidation and agreed to try and squeeze in a piece of pie.

When the pie came out, the filling was a pale green color. An excellent start, no artificial colorings to make it look "lime green." The taste of the pie was amazing. It was creamy and tangy without being too tart. It was delicious. Despite being full, I managed to completely clean my plate. It was the perfect end to what had been a really enjoyable and relaxing afternoon and evening.

I have tried to replicate the taste of the key lime pie that I had at the Palm Pavilion, but I have to admit it has been a process of trial and error. So instead, the recipe I have included here is more sympathetic to the original recipe, with the use of raw egg and relying on souring to "cook" the pie. This recipe is therefore not suitable for the very young, pregnant women, the elderly, or those with weak immune systems. An alternative would be to buy pasteurized egg yolks (available in supermarkets in some countries), or to cook the pie in a medium oven for twenty minutes (although I have never personally tried this). Another possibility would be to omit the eggs entirely. However, the pie will need to be baked so that the filling sets.

There are a lot of variations to the recipe. Apart from omitting the eggs, other variations include folding in whipped cream, which reduces the tartness and richness of the filling, or using more limes and lime zest to make the pie tangier. The egg whites can also be used to create a meringue topping on the pie.

The Hungry Traveller's Key Lime Pie – serves 8

Shopping List

    7 tbsp. butter

    250g (0.55 lb.) Digestive Biscuits/Graham crackers

    4 fresh limes

    4 large egg yolks

    400g (1.3 cups) sweetened condensed milk

Preparation

Step 1:

Line the base and sides of a 7 to 8 inch flan tin with baking paper.

Step 2:

Melt the butter in a pan over a low heat. Using a food processor, break down the biscuits into fine crumb and mix in the butter.

Step 3:

Press the mixture over the base and sides of the lined tin. Place in the fridge until the base is set.

Step 4:

Squeeze the juice from the limes.

Step 5:

Beat the egg yolks. Slowly add the condensed milk to the eggs and continue beating together the ingredients. Fold in the lime juice and pour the mixture onto the base.

Step 6:

Refrigerate for approximately three hours until the pie has set.

Step 7:

Serve with whipped cream.

A Final Word

Sometimes travel can be a life-changing experience. You don't always have to trek through mountains and jungle or travel halfway across a continent.

You can learn a lot about yourself by doing very little and just staring out across the sea for a couple of weeks, alone with your thoughts. I am not sure if I learned anything new about myself, but I did remember things about myself. Things that had become forgotten and had become deeply buried by my day to day existence.

I had spent too long doing what I thought was expected, and all I had was a mortgage and a job that was taking over my life and making me miserable.

It was time to do something I wanted to do with my life.

When I returned from my two weeks of reflection by the beach, I quit my job without having any idea of what I wanted to do next. All I knew was that it was the right decision to make and probably a decision that was long overdue.

Maybe I'll write a book…

References

Singapore

Chew, Ernest (1991). Lee, Edwin. Ed. *A History of Singapore,* Oxford University Press.

King, Rodney (2008). *The Singapore Miracle, Myth and Reality*, Insight Press.

Shenon, Philip (10 October 1991). *Singapore Journal; Back to Somerset Maugham and Life's Seamy Side.* The New York Times.

Rome, Italy

BBC.co.uk. *BBC's History of the Colosseum.* [Accessed October 2011]

Claridge, Amanda (1988). *Rome, Oxford Archaeological Guides, Oxford Oxfordshire,* Oxford University Press.

MacDonald, William. L (1976). *The Pantheon: Design, Meaning and Progeny,* Cambridge, MA: Harvard University Press.

Roth, Leland M (1993). *Understanding Architecture: Its Elements, History and Meaning* (First ed.). Boulder, CO: Westview Press.

Scarre, Chris (1995). *The Penguin Historical Atlas of Ancient Rome.* London, Penguin Books.

Brighton, England

Beevers, David (2008). *The Royal Pavilion, Brighton: Souvenir Guide and Catalogue.*

Carder, Timothy (1990). *The Encyclopaedia of Brighton*, S127 East Sussex County Libraries.

Zanzibar, Tanzania

http://www.wikipedia.org/wiki/Zanzibar [Accessed October 2011]

http://www.zanzibar-travel-guide.com/bradt.guide.asp [Accessed October 2011]

http://www.wikipedia.org/wiki/Stone_town [Accessed October 2011]

http://www.zanzibar.cc/stonetown [Accessed October 2011]

MacKenzie, D.N (2005). A *Concise Pahlavi Dictionary. London & New York,* Routledge Curzon.

Morocco

http://www.wikipedia.org/wiki/Ait_Benhaddou [Accessed November 2011]

Santorini, Greece

Pellegrino, Charles (1991) *Unearthing Atlantis – An Archaeological Odyssey*, Vintage Books.

Phytikas, Michael. *The South Aegean Active Volcanic Arc: Present Knowledge and Future Perspectives.*

http://www.wikipedia.org/wiki/Santorini [Accessed November 2011]

Sydney, Australia

"*Regional Population Growth, Australia, 2009-10.*"
Australian Bureau of Statistics (31 March 2011).
http://www.doyles.com.au [Accessed November 2011]

Ireland

Kelly, Eamonn (2009). *The Cliffs of Moher*, Matt Kelly.
Rider, M.H (1974). *The Namurian of West County Clare.*

Phnom Penh, Cambodia

Chandler, David (1999). *Voices from S-21; Terror and History Inside Pol-Pot's Secret Prison*, University of California Press.
Scheffer, David; Chhang. Youk. *Historical Overview of the Khmer Rouge*. Cambodia Tribunal Monitor.

http://wikipedia.org/wiki/Khmer_Rouge [Accessed December 2011]
http://www.wikipedia.org/wiki/Tuol_Sleng_Genocide_Museum [Accessed December 2011]

New York & Philadelphia, USA

http://www.wikipedia.org/wiki/Bryant_Park [Accessed December 2011]

Kanchanaburi, Thailand

Kinvig, Clifford (1992). *River Kwai Railway: The Story of the Burma-Siam Railway*. London, Brassey's.

http://www.wikipedia.org/wiki/The_Burma_Railway [Accessed December 2011]

http://www.wikipedia.org/wiki/Hellfire_Pass [Accessed December 2011]

Wattle Publishing

Wattle Publishing is an independent
publishing house based in London.
We publish fiction and non-fiction
works in a range of categories.

'Join us' on Twitter: @wattlepub

'Like us' on Facebook: Wattle Publishing

www.wattlepublishing.com